THE WORLD OF

Fishing for
Largemouth
Bass

SINCE 1895

FIELD&
STREAM

THE SOUL OF THE AMERICAN OUTDOORS

P9-AGC-898

CREATIVE
PUBLISHING
international

MINNETONKA, MINNESOTA

Field & Stream
The World of Fishing for Largemouth Bass

Introduction by Slaton L. White, Managing Editor, FIELD & STREAM

President: Iain Macfarlane
Group Director, Book Development: Zoe Graul
Director, Creative Development: Lisa Rosenthal
Executive Managing Editor: Elaine Perry

Executive Editor, Outdoor Group: Don Oster
Project Leader and Article Editor: David R. Maas
Managing Editor: Denise Bornhausen
Associate Creative Director: Brad Springer
Art Directors: Joe Fahey, Dave Schelitzche
Photo Researcher: Angie Spann
Copy Editor: Janice Cauley
Desktop Publishing Specialist: Laurie Kristensen
Publishing Production Manager: Stasia Dorn
Cover Photo: Bill Lindner

Special thanks to: Jason E. Klein, President, FIELD & STREAM; Duncan Barnes,
Slaton L. White, and the staff of FIELD & STREAM magazine

Contributing Photographers: Joe Albea, Grady Allen, Bob Brister, Jim Dean, Joe Doggett,
Mark Hicks, Bill Lindner, David J. Sams/Texas Inprint, Ken Schultz, Dave Whitlock

Contributing Illustrators: John F. Eggert, Dale Glasgow & Associates, W. Hardbark
McLoughlin, Doug Schermer, Slim Films

Printed on American Paper
03 02 01 00 99 / 5 4 3 2 1

Library of Congress Cataloging–in–Publication Data

Field & Stream : the world of fishing for largemouth bass/from the editors of
    Field & Stream and Creative Publishing international, Inc.
        p. cm.
    ISBN 0–86573–090–3 (hard cover) . – – ISBN 0–86573–091–1 (softcover)
    1. Largemouth bass fishing. I. Creative Publishing International.
    II. Field & stream. III. Title: Fishing for largemouth bass.
    SH681.W66 1999
    799. 1'77388– –dc21   98–48228

Table of Contents

Introduction

AMERICA'S FISH? NO QUESTION, it's the largemouth bass. Found from multi-armed impoundments to farm ponds small enough to spit across—the bass is as American as, well, apple pie. The ready availability of this democratic fish is one reason it has become the country's number-one gamefish, but that in itself doesn't fully explain the extraordinary cult of bass fishing.

There's something else. It's the nature of the largemouth bass. A friend of mine once wrote, "The fish is a brawler, a potbellied thug with no respect for decency or refinement. Ain't that great!" True. The largemouth has also been characterized as "The Mouth That Swims," no doubt a tribute to its voracious appetite.

The largemouth is at its brawling best when it zeros in on some hapless offering—and like many anglers, I live for that strike. When a bass commits to a lure, the result is pure mayhem—a violent head slam. The hit keeps us coming back for more.

From its founding in 1895, FIELD & STREAM— the largest, most widely read outdoor magazine in the world—has reported on the phenomenon of bass fishing. In the early days, the magazine served as a clearinghouse of information for a fish that was still considered by many to be a regional (read Southern) specialty. In the 1920s, the fishing editor devoted much of his allotted space to comprehensive dissertations on the proper methods of catching the black bass, or green trout, as the fish was also known in those days.

The editor also answered reader mail. Many of the questions dealt with live bait—and one of the most-asked questions concerned a small crustacean known variously as the crawdad, crawfish, or crayfish. Patiently, the fishing editor explained these were one and the same—and a choice bait for largemouths. Back then, when gamefish and baitfish went by a constellation of confusing local names, this was important reader service.

Bass fishing took its "Great Leap Forward" after World War II. A tidal wave of dam building created reservoirs where bass (and the forage they needed to feed upon) thrived, and the emerging interstate highway system made it easier than ever to get to new bass waters. In 1941, Peter Barrett (later Executive Editor at FIELD & STREAM) wrote about a new type of fishing tackle of European design. It was called spinning, and when spinning reels reached our shores in 1947, the sport was revolutionized. A few years later, the legendary A.J. McClane alerted FIELD & STREAM readers to another sea change in tackle—a new type of artificial lure called the plastic worm.

Since then, bass fishing has continued to grow by leaps and bounds to become the dominant form of freshwater fishing in America. And FIELD & STREAM has continued to report on the major developments in bass fishing, ranging from the technological (graphite rods, graph recorders, braided "superlines") to the sociological (the rise of professional bass fishing, the shift in emphasis from live bait to artificial lures, and the ascent of catch-and-release fishing).

Whatever the trend, FIELD & STREAM has always assigned its best writers to cover it. And this book is a collection of the best of the best.

The articles have been arranged into four sections. The first is "America's Fish." Here you'll find a compelling selection of articles that discuss the traditions of this great sport. Though each writer approaches the bass from a unique viewpoint, ultimately each asks the same question: "Why does the largemouth bass appeal so strongly to anglers?"

The second section is "Bass Through the Seasons." In many states, bass fishing is now year-round sport, and the fishing changes in accordance to the season. An approach that works in the lazy, hazy days of summer doesn't stand a snowball's chance when the bottom falls out of the thermometer. It pays to know the difference.

The third section is "Bass Fishing Techniques." This is basic nuts and bolts, but with a difference. You'll benefit from the hard-won experience of each author as some of the all-time lures and techniques are dissected and amplified. And though no writer can guarantee success, these are all methods that have stood the test of time.

The fourth and final section is "Special Situations." Here, you'll encounter a number of specific bass fishing problems—and how to overcome each. Bass fishing is often like a puzzle—and when you finally are able to fit in all the pieces, the complete picture is truly a blueprint for success.

Our grandfathers may not recognize how we fish for bass these days—graphite rods, GPS-based electronics, and metal-flake boats powered by outsized outboards would no doubt confound anyone who came of age with steel rods and black cotton line. But the old men would no doubt understand our continuing passion for the sport. Like them, we are still seduced by a swirl and a take. It's a siren call from another world, and after all these years, the message is still plain: *I am wild, I am free, take me if you can.*

Slaton L. White,
Managing Editor, FIELD & STREAM

America's Fish

Bass fishing is an American anomaly. It is one of the most modern forms of fishing—utilizing the very latest in high-tech gear and refined techniques—and yet, it is also one of the most traditional, using time-tested tactics and tackle. The tie that binds these two approaches is the fish, which responds in equal measure to both.

The modern bass fisherman is often suspended between these two parallel universes, and the smart angler recognizes that a visit to the past can enrich the present. Sometimes, stepping out of the modern fast lane can lead to the rediscovery of an old, dust-covered lure that can still turn on bass. Or, the slow lane may simply be a refreshing (and surprisingly effective) pause from modern run-and-gun tactics. In either case, you'll find that a perusal of the traditions of bass fishing, the subject of the following articles, will help explain why this fish matters to so many of us.

SINCE 1895

FIELD & STREAM

THE SOUL OF THE AMERICAN OUTDOORS

By Keith McCafferty

BRENT'S
Bass

HOPEFULLY, THE FISHING TRIP WOULD BE THE STUFF OF WHICH MEMORIES ARE MADE——IF NOT FOR THE BOY, THEN MAYBE FOR THE MAN HE WOULD BECOME.

"TIME TO GO FISHING," I said in a soft voice. I reached over and shook the small hills the boys made in their sleeping bags. "Come on now, the fish are awake."

I flicked on my flashlight, dressed quietly, and stepped outside the tent. *Give them a minute,* I thought. Overhead, the stars were still hard. The arm of the lake was buried under a thick fog. I knew it would be 90 degrees before noon. But this far north, this far into August, autumn stirred in its sleep every morning to silver the grass with frost.

The lantern hissed and caught. I brought it into the tent, where it threw its monstrous shadow against the canvas and brought frowns to the boys' faces.

"Tom, do you want to go fish with me?" My son shook his head and wiggled in his sleeping bag.

"Brent, time to get up." There was no response.

"Men!" I said sternly. "The day has broke and the leviathan awaits."

Ten minutes later I held two cold hands on the walk down to the water. The boys sat down on the frosted aluminum seats in the johnboat, their watch caps pulled down to their eyebrows, their hands in their pockets, their hearts still back up the hill, where they'd have slept past sunrise had I let them. Sometimes what a boy says he wants to do and what he really wants to do are not the same thing, especially if the grand talk of fishing was kindled by the evening fire, with morning as uncomprehendingly distant as the last light on the horizon.

I shoved my oars into the gravel and I pushed off the shore. The oar blades came up smoking with fog and we were swallowed into the lake.

"Okay, men," I said. "Get those plugs in the water."

Tom reached for his rod and sent an old balsa-wood Rapala out with a two-fisted cast. It made a lonely splash in the mist.

"Brent, don't you want to fish? This is the best time."

He shook his head and sniffed his red nose. "My hands are too cold," he said. I took his spinning rod and cast out. Maybe if I could catch a bass on his rod, he'd change his mind. You couldn't predict Brent. He was seven, a year younger than Tom, but big for his age. He was rough and all wound up, but sometimes he could be a scared kid, scared of most anything and particularly of me.

My brother Kevin had wanted Brent to come camping with me. "You'll catch a big fish if you go with Uncle Keith," he persuaded him, and he'd agreed to go, finally, only because of

Tom. I promised myself to be on my best behavior and try not to tease him.

But Brent was such a sensitive child and I was such a big child that I couldn't resist. And since I couldn't change, Brent took cover with Tom whenever I'd raise an eyebrow and tell them about the bear track outside the tent, or some other nonsense I'd dream up. Tom would look at him and rather sadly shake his head. Brent would defiantly say, "No, there isn't!" just as his lip would begin to quiver, and then his voice would chime in shrilly a half-step after Tom's in declaring me a "big fat hairy Belucca."

So in all matters of disagreement, teasing, and ordering about they became the good guys and I was the big fat whatever, which made for a situation we could all live with and one with which I was patently familiar. This mock warfare helped Brent keep his distance from me, however, which was something I didn't want, the unstated purpose of the trip being to bring us closer together. An idea began to take root that if only he could catch a big fish, that barrier might crack a little. But Brent was having bad luck; he hadn't caught a bass the first morning of the trip when Tom took three, he hadn't caught one yesterday, and now on our third and last morning, he was keeping his hands in his pockets. Tom was still casting, but without spirit or hope. The day before yesterday might as well have been last year in boy time.

"I got the lure on your rod that Tom caught the bass with Monday," I said to Brent. "You watch, now, and I'll get one."

Sometimes miracles don't come from above. This one rose from down under and swirled at the surface, leapt clear at the bite of the hook, and dove back down to bore into the coontail fronds. I kept the rod high and kept him coming. The water felt warm to the touch, and then the bass was in the boat, a long frond of weed trailing from the lure down past his tail. I worked the treble free and slipped the largemouth, which was about 14 inches long,

I have caught two bass and they have caught me, a small voice throbbed in the back of my mind.

back into the warm water. "You want to try now?" Brent nodded his head yes and I handed him the rod.

"Cast the lines, men," I said, and they did so with such fervor that both plugs smacked down no more than 10 feet from the boat. I knew then I had myself some bass fishermen. It's a wonder what one fish will do.

During this time, we had drifted at sea, as it were. To the distant east, the teeth of the Swan mountain range had defined themselves above the fog, but below the timberline all was lost. As for the fishing, this was a matter of little consequence. The lake was of uniform depth here at the outlet, and fraught with weeds and lilies, and at this hour the bass cruised anywhere and everywhere. Just the right kind of fishing for boys of their age, whose plugs fell as aimlessly as the baseballs they threw from the outfield in Little League.

"I got one!" It was Tom, and my heart sank at the same instant it rose. Why couldn't Brent catch one? "Keep him coming. If he gets down in the weeds we'll lose him."

"I am, I am," said Tom. "Oh, he's going to get away. He's too big for me." For Tom, the world fell apart when he hooked a fish.

"Brent?" I yelled. "Your rod's bent over. Reel!"

"It's just a weed," Brent said. He was looking out in the direction of Tom's fish.

"Reel, for crise sakes!" Out in the mist, the water itself seemed to have exploded. Again the fish jumped, and it seemed to dawn on Brent that maybe he did indeed have one on.

It was chaos. Tom's bass had bored underneath the boat and was pulling hard, yanking the rod tip underwater. Brent's rod was doubled over Tom's shoulder. And the boat was shaking. There was little I could do but that which all fathers do best. Yell orders.

"Keep the rod tip up! Swing your rod over, Brent!"

"Ow!" Tom howled. Brent's rod had swept him across the face and knocked his hat into the water.

"He's going to get away. I know it. Daddy, do something."

I had the net out and dug it under the surface. Up came Tom's bass. One down and one to go. But the hooks of the lure were attached not only to the fish's mouth but also to the meshes. I fumbled my hand down into the net to free the trebles and in an instant my finger was caught past the barb. Undaunted—for the point of this trip was to catch Brent a bass, and catch it we would—I reached my free arm over the side of the boat and hauled Brent's bass out in one fell motion, my thumb and forefinger clamped onto its lip. The swinging rear treble of the plug caught under my wedding ring and lodged, miraculously, without impaling the tender flesh.

"Yahoo!" Brent said, and jerked his rod with an excited gesture. The bass twisted its muscled sides. My finger shot forward 3 inches and the hook drove home. Out on the lake a loon laughed hysterically while the smiles of two small boys drew instantly into frightened Os. I will not ruin this moment for them, I told myself. So I forced a grin while all else subsided into the grimmest of silence. A strong white heat radiated outward from my two hands, brought dizziness to my head, then drained back down to the fingertips to pulse once and once more. *I have caught two bass and they have caught me,* a small voice throbbed in the back of my mind. It seemed like an eternity passed until the hooks came free.

I had the presence of mind to snap a couple of photographs, one bass in the net, another on the boat bottom, while a trickle of my blood zigged down past the shutter and ran across the lens. I knew that in time the morning would come to transcend the tragedy of my fingers. After all, Brent's bass must have weighed 3 pounds and Tom's was not much smaller. Finally, the fish were slipped back into the water. We hooked my son's hat off the surface with a rod tip and I gingerly beat the oars for shore. But we were caught in the current at the outlet of the lake, more than a quarter mile from camp, and I do not think the boat made progress so much as the land came home.

———— ✠ ————

BACK AT THE tent, I made breakfast with a whistle and a wince. Already Brent seemed to have forgotten the bass. He and Tom were preoccupied upending cones of sand to build castles and scooping out moats that drained down to the shallows. Later that day, when we rowed back out into the sunshine and dropped worms overboard for perch, they became atwitter with nerves at the dancing of the bobbers. They never tired of swinging 4-inch fish into the boat. It seemed to bring them much more satisfaction than they'd had flinging plugs into the mist with cold hands, and with the exception of one strike apiece, drawing forth nothing in return but the balsa wood minnows they had cast.

The photos I took of the bass came out so dark that the film lab would not develop them. Now that I've had time to reflect, it seems only appropriate that the perch photos are clear and sharp, and the smiles on the boy's faces are from here to tomorrow.

Children show so little remembrance of the things we hope will be precious to them. They live for the moment and for the moments that lie ahead. It is only when we are adults that we look back, and just as Brent's bass meant more to me than it did to him at the time, it is my hope that the fish will secure a better foothold in his memory somewhere down the line. I do know that he has not entirely forgotten. My brother called me on the phone the other day, and he mentioned that they'd been watching a fishing program on television, and when the fella hauled a bass over the stern, Brent said to him, "Phooeey, I caught a bigger one with Uncle Keith." My brother said the bass looked to be 5 pounds.

"Why, he's a fisherman already," I told him.

By Joe Doggett

America's FISH

IF THE LARGEMOUTH WERE HUMAN, IT WOULD
INVITE YOU TO STEP OUT OF THE BAR AND
SETTLE THINGS WITH FISTS, KNIVES, OR CLUBS.

THE LARGEMOUTH
black bass may be the most
popular sport fish in the United States,
but it is a mauler and a brawler, a potbellied
thug with no respect for decency or refinement.
This is a fish of questionable origin.

The bass is, inherently, a creature of the
swamp. *Micropterus* is the mate of the alligator
and the gar, the otter and the cottonmouth—
all the things that splash and swirl in the dark.
No amount of finishing can alter or rehabili-
tate this breeding. Ain't that great!

Brother bass is native to the backwaters of
the South, but today's expanded range includes
the entire Lower 48 and numerous foreign
flags. The bass is a survivor. I once caught a
bass named Henry from a bathtub. And, while
that incident might reveal a certain bushness in
my makeup, it illustrates an adaptability
uncommon among gamefish species. Virtually
any source of fresh or brackish water with a
pollution level this side of spontaneous flash
point can harbor bass. Most are stocked in
respectable waters with names—the major
reservoirs and lakes—but never discount the
turbid drainage ditch or the scummy slough.

Wherever our bass is found, it remains
unreconstructed. It brings from the black water
a swashbuckling attitude and the legacy of the
big hit. The largemouth, as its name suggests,
boasts great capacity for topwater terrorism. A
snook or a jungle *pavon* might teach a sow bass a
few lessons in bad manners, but no native
freshwater fish can equal the wound-up surface
strike. When its goggle eyes and surly lips rise

to the surface, the bad vibes scatter with the spray. This fish is a killer.

When the hook is set, the lunker carries its bad act back home, into the shadowed canopies of weeds and the back alleys of logs. It's over, one way or the other, within moments. A plug rod is a stiff-arm. You rear back with a vicious power sweep and crank hard and fast, trying to turn the head as the fish dives and roots for cover. A fly rod is a lever. You don't forfeit the advantage by attempting to get the fish "on the reel." Such a conventional free rein encourages the time and slack for the fish to obtain snags and wraps. You double the rod and lock the line against the grip and start hauling—and the devil take the incoming coils. By either method, increments are surrendered grudgingly, if at all. This is no place for finesse; it is a heavyweight bout with both combatants swinging knockout punches while the Marquis of Queensberry lies dazed and bleeding in the lily pads.

You have to get after it; there's no other way to win, assuming a lunker is hooked amid the tangled environs it favors. I reckon sand flats are fine for bonefish, but don't look for many big bass in the open. And don't expect them to play fair.

The largemouth prefers to get down and dirty, but it is capable of heroic and repeated leaps. A big fish is most apt to jump when levered to the top, or if a lure is hung deep in its gaping maw. A good old fashioned gill wallowing, fin-bristling, coot-scattering emergence is as bold an image as exists in fishing.

The bass, despite its bluntness and roundness, is a good-looking fish. The greens and golds and silvers swell with pride and the fins are the right size. So are the scales—not too coarse like a carp's, not too slick like a catfish's skin. It wears its weight well; indeed, a bass without girth is poor.

But this fish is more than a handsome widebody. The largemouth, for all its brute tactics and aggressive nature, is a fish of substance. It is intelligent and fickle, capable of repeatedly confounding some of the finest talent that angling has known. It is a sad mistake—one usually reflected through an empty livewell—to assume that because the largemouth is ruthless and gluttonous, it is not discriminating. To say that the bass is dull, never selective, is to have your head stuck in the nearest nutria hole.

Once, I watched from a lighted dock as midnight bass fed on hatching mayflies. As the ethereal insects fluttered and danced, 3- to 5-pound bass drifted ghostlike to sip the dainty offerings. The usual entreaties of clattering spinnerbaits, sputtering topwater plugs, and fluttering crankbaits were met with magnificent disregard while, repeatedly, a size 10 sulfur dun drew confident rises. The incident was a revelation, and a reminder that the bass is a more complex study than the heavy jaw and thick belly might suggest.

I was shocked. It was as if back at the marina, beyond the bar with the icy longnecks and the twangy juke box and salty pork skins, behind the door with the tractor pull calendar, Bubba and Billy Ray were seated with demitasses, peering through lorgnettes at selected works of Middle English poets. The largemouth is rough, often unpolished, but a fish of undeniable vitality and surprising contrast. It often is more than it seems. That is appropriate for America's fish.

By Bill Heavey

BASS LAND

THIS SPECIAL WORLD,
WHERE WHAT YOU SEE
IS WHAT YOU WANT, IS
A COZY PLACE FOR
THOSE WHO WILLINGLY
SUSPEND THEIR BELIEF.

I'VE JUST BUSTLED INTO my boss's office like the Energizer Bunny, had him sign off on a few things to pump his ego, asked his advice on several matters I've already settled, and hurried out as if my one sorrow in life is that there aren't more hours in the day to do his bidding. Now I'm back in my office, computer burning like one of those convenience-store fire logs, papers scattered strategically across my desk so that you have to look hard to see what I'm really doing. An innocent man serving 9-to-5 in the work force until his conviction is overturned needs an occasional break. Me, I'm going catalog fishing.

I open up the glossy 420-page four-color wish-book and it's like someone's squirting Hawg Scent directly into my imagination. It's part Publisher's Clearing House and part Disneyland, a place where big fish happen to little people and our favorite myths are real. Look, here's a little woman in her fifties from Weedsport, New York, holding up a tiger muskie with a head the size of a coal shovel. How'd she get that sucker into the boat? Over here are a couple of guys who look like they've just been hit with a stun gun, holding up bass so fat they would have exploded if somebody hadn't caught them that very day. And here comes a retired policeman who dredged up a Castaic Lake lunker just a couple of pounds shy of that 22-pound 4-ounce record. It doesn't look like a bass with its mouth open; it looks like the hole in your clothes dryer with gill plates and fins attached. Hey, it coulda been you or me. I got the very same manufacturer's jig and garlic-scented sparkle frog trailer in my box right now.

I like it in here. It's cozy. All my favorite bassin' pals are right between these shellacked covers. Like Ole Uncle Buddy holding up a stringer of stone-dead crappies, with two beautiful children from the talent agency who would file a lawsuit if forced to touch an actual fish. And those two dudes, with chins like Superman's and headlight teeth, wearing teal and persimmon "fishing shirts," sitting in heavy hydrilla aboard a boat cleaner than a surgical hospital, with Mayan-inspired hieroglyphs on the side, who have managed simultaneous hookups of fish the size of Andre the Giant. They both look kinda pleased, as well they should.

I love these pictures. I want them to be true. I want one of those once-in-five-years hookups, and that gruff uncle with the gold-plated heart to keep the kids away from me

while I'm fishing. Hey, I don't just *want* these things; I *deserve* them. That $200 spinning reel with seven stainless-steel ball bearings already endorsed by NASA in case there are bass in deep space. I'm *entitled* to that, along with the commemorative bait-caster and all those new lures endorsed by bass pros as "the fishgettin'est piece (titanium, Naugahyde, or high-molecular-weight thermo-setting polymer) I've ever tied on a line!" I must have the banana-scented grubs and lures that fly away from me and do-nothing lures with cooked-in pork fat and goop that simulates the "real molting fluid" of crayfish so that my sportsmanlike artificial lure is twice as enticing as live bait. I covet the tandem Willowleaf/Colorado spinnerbaits hand-hammered by mad Swiss elves until they gleam in the dark and Teflon-coated hooks so sharp you can splice genes with 'em. My head is swimming under the strain of all the things I long to own.

And then, for just a second, there is a moment of calm, like when the roller coaster runs out of momentum just as you crest the Big Rock Candy Mountain, or that twinkling when you suddenly notice that the wind you've been casting into all day has blown itself out. I take a deep breath, remembering who and what I am. I ask myself, *Do I really need all this stuff?* I mean in my heart of hearts. There is a nanosecond of deep reflection before the answer comes back fast and straight as truth's arrow: Damn *right* I do! All of it! I need hook bonnets! I need that graphite rod with the Portuguese cork handle so sensitive it'll pull you overboard if a dragonfly lands on the tip, and the camouflage lockback knife with Parkerized blade I'll lose the first time I set it down on the ground between my feet. Never mind that some of the new soft jerk baits look like what happens if you step on a tube of toothpaste by mistake. Never mind that I don't need a lure retriever shaped like a hound dog or glasses with an FM radio built in or a Nostalgia Tin of last year's lures. I *want* these things. I want them almost bad enough to pay real money for them.

My phone rings. It's my boss. He wants to know if I meant to give him a coupon for five bucks off a self-cleaning fish scaler that plugs into his car lighter. Suddenly I'm back from Bass Fantasy Land, back with my computer and my 9-to-5. But now I'm ready for a *real* break in the routine.

Three weeks later it's the second day of a two-day solo canoe float down the upper part of my favorite bass stream. Last night I lay on the sand before pitching my tent and wiggled around to hollow out places for my shoulders, hips, and spine. I breaststroked in place while the current's fingers stroked the kinks out of my body, and with the help of dry pine needles got a fire going with my first match. I rubbed garlic cloves over a small steak and cooked it rare, washed it down with two cans of beer, and had three peaches for dessert. Then the summer night sounds came up behind the river's singing, and I watched the embers fade until they looked like the lights of an orange city far below me.

This morning, poking around in thigh-deep water downstream, I found a ledge below which three identical 14-inch bass fell for a smoke-white grub on a 1/16-inch jighead. Two shook their heads at me in anger as they sputtered over the surface like drops of oil in a hot pan. The third fish dove deep, then rocketed north to execute a series of nearly splashless back flips, as if the key to throwing the hook lay in altitude alone. It had taken me a day to leave the world of timesheets and deodorant behind, but this morning it felt like the line to

When the reality out there proves to be too much, retreat to Bass Land—a dream world designed especially for you.

each fish ran through the rod, up my arms, and tightened around something in my chest. Now I look up as a pair of kingfishers flies close patrol, keeping the shallows honest, and up high a red-shouldered hawk is circling, waiting for any snake, frog, or crayfish to make a mistake. I decide to rest the spot and try it with a different lure after breaking camp.

Now I'm sitting on my island with my feet in the river, sun beating down on me. I like this place, the river splitting around it as if to seal it off from the outside world. And I know that as soon as I get in the canoe the trip's half over. I fuss with my tackle—sharpening hooks and cleaning yesterday's spider webs and crud out of rod guides. As I pull a new floater/diver crankbait from its plastic lamination, the flier inside helicopters down. It tells me where to send my check for a polyester hat, a sportsman's terrycloth towel, and a patch to sew on my shirt. What seemed so seductive under fluorescent light is absurd out here, a slice of chemically processed tree with ink stains on it. I crumple it up and put it on last night's ashes, cover it with twigs, and strike a match to start water for a final cup of coffee. The plastic flares like a matchhead, the flier wrinkles and blackens, and I'm glad the packaging hasn't gone to waste. I tie the lure on, flattening the barbs with the forceps I keep around my neck. It's time to get back on the water and see who's interested in this thing.

By Bob Brister

Best Little Bass Baits from
TEXAS

THE LAYFIELD
BROTHERS' LURES
COULD TURN BEGINNERS
INTO NEAR-EXPERTS,
AND EXPERTS INTO
BASSING LEGENDS.

*I*T WAS BITTER COLD on Trinidad Lake in east-central Texas, and schools of shad were swarming into the heated current boiling out of Texas Power & Light Company's generators. A lot of bass were already in the warm water, waiting in ambush around a submerged stump at the edge of casting range. Occasionally, the surface would detonate into multiple showers of silvery baitfish.

Three shivering teenagers casting from the abutment of No. 1 bridge were having little better luck than the shad. Pearl Harbor had been bombed a couple of months before, and fears of sabotage had shut down access to the waters near the plant. We couldn't reach the ambush stump with our gear-groaning direct-drive reels, and even when we came close, our big plugs often turned on their sides and refused to run right in the swift cross currents. In those days, there were very few plugs small enough to imitate shad.

So we watched with considerable interest when a couple of fellows in Fedora hats walked up. At the ends of their rods dangled little pearl-colored plugs no longer than a redhorse minnow. The man in the gray

Fedora stepped down to the water's edge and casually dropped an incredible long cast beyond the stump. He let his plug sink a second or so, and began a slow retrieve. Immediately his rod bent and a frisky 3-pound bass came up to jump.

"Throw in behind me, Cotton," he yelled to the one in the black hat. "Probably a school in there. This 'un took it before it ever got to the stump."

Then it dawned on me. These had to be the lure-making Layfield brothers from the Powell community not far from my home town of Kerens. People came from all over the country to buy the expensive (85 cents at Bain's

hardware), patented plugs whittled out by Jester Layfield. His brother Floyd (Cotton) was rumored to have some secret topwater lure he wouldn't even fish with in public until his own patents were granted.

They for sure knew how to fish. Taking turns casting to the stump, they caught five bass on their first seven casts. And if a strike didn't come at the stump, they'd crank as fast as their old Shakespeare Marhoff reels would go, racing the lures back through nonproductive water to save time for the next cast. Even at top speed, the little lures ran perfectly straight, wiggling tighter and harder the faster they were pulled. I watched them as a physics student might have studied Einstein. And when the one in the gray hat sat down to smoke a cigarette—waiting for more bass to move in around the ambush stump—I hunkered down beside him and began asking a million questions. Surprisingly, considering the status of a high-school freshman in 1942 who hadn't made the football team, he answered every one.

"The shape of the body and the weight of the spoon is mostly what makes 'em run straight," he explained. (He called the plug's diving lip a spoon then, just as he does now at age eighty-six.) "The spoon needs to be long enough that when it comes to a log or somethin' it hits first and tips the hind end of the bait over without hanging up."

That's no novel idea nowadays, but it surely was then. In fact, he showed me the drop of solder he put on the ring of the front set of treble hooks to keep them from swinging too far forward and hanging obstructions as the plug flipped over.

"You can fish this little sucker right over logs or brush, places where you'd hang up those store-bought baits of yours ever' time," he said proudly. "An' you cain't pull one of my baits fast enough to make it turn over and quit. These here are Goin' Jessies."

I told him they sure enough were, and if I could ever afford 'em, that's all I'd fish with, except for my fly-rod poppers or, sometimes a Shimmy Wiggler in thick moss.

"Well," he chuckled, reaching into his pocket and taking another pearl-colored plug from a water-stained cardboard box, "if you can throw this 'un out to that stump yonder, I'll give it to you."

I nearly choked and got a semi-fizzle backlash toward the end of the cast. But the little plug flew heavily for its size, just far enough to drop straight down upon the stump, where it should have snagged, had not a bass wrapped its jaws around the hooks in the nick of time.

That was the start of a friendship, and an education in bass fishing, that has lasted more than half a century. For three more high-school years I fished with the Layfields, learning more than I'd ever thought there was to know about bass. Although they were dirt farmers emerging from the hard times of the Depression, they found plenty of time to fish. And they were absolute maestros at the art of sidearming deadly accurate casts beneath overhanging brush, catching bass where most fishermen would never dare to send a lure.

Jess had been carving out his plugs with a pocketknife since the early 1920s, and his wife Mary Beth painted them. They had saved enough money to pay attorney fees to patent the original lure in 1939. Shortly thereafter, Jess came up with the most efficient system yet devised for combining the then-new Fred Arbogast rubber skirt with a wiggling plug. Rather than hanging the skirt on the plug's tail,

Unlike today's frog, this little hummer walked. And when bass blew up through the salad, they were definitely trying to kill it.

thus killing some of its wiggle (as Arbogast did with the Hula Dancer), Layfield positioned the skirt in a groove cut just behind the head of his plugs. This way the lure and skirt could wiggle independently, the skirt lagging a half-wiggle behind due to water resistance.

The result was an incredibly snaky, pollywoggish wiggle in a slow-settling plug he called the Skirt Bait. Start the retrieve and the skirt would be compressed by water pressure to resemble a swimming tail. Stop momentarily and it would slowly settle, the skirt tails fanning out over its back like the legs of some insect. It murdered bass around shorelines, and still will, particularly on smaller lakes and farm ponds.

Cotton, meanwhile, was perfecting a top-water lure that would walk water. Shaped something like a banjo (wide at the head to fend off weeds and brush), it had a little axle that turned inside a brass bushing in its underbelly. At either end of that axle were cupped, double-bladed paddlewheels soldered solidly to the shaft and offset so that one paddle would always be in the water to keep the shaft rotating. The upturned single hook was carried behind and above its back (like a scorpion's stinger) and the underside was smooth to slide over brush or vegetation. It could be walked slowly over a solid mat of surface vegetation, sort of hippity-hopping from side to side as the paddles turned, and bass would blast right up through solid weeds trying to kill the thing. If retrieved slowly in open water, the paddlewheels purred; if speeded up, they buzzed like an angry bee, apparently at a sound frequency that bass could perceive from some distance away.

I first saw that proven during a bronzely beautiful October sunset while waiting for doves to come to water on Kerens City Lake. Cotton was casting down a narrow lane between two patches of water lilies, making the lure buzz back over its own row of bubbles time after time. About every two dozen throws a bass would blow up in the lane of reflected sunset. I watched one of those fish bulge water coming from far back in the vegetation. Two casts later he finally homed in on it and blasted water all over Cotton's khakis.

"That buzzin' noise kind of tolls 'em out of bad places," Cotton noted, puffing his pipe merrily. "I could fish it right over that thick stuff, but a big bass is too likely to wrap up and break off. Besides, I like to call 'em to me."

This was long before today's buzzbaits or, for that matter, before the popularity of the plastic worm or skirted spinnerbait. The Layfields had built a better fish trap—three in fact—but the world was not exactly beating a path to their door.

I remember how excited they were when some officials of a major lure company came down to see a demonstration of their lure. Jess and two of his brothers so badly outfished the factory people that he was confident they'd put his plugs into production, pay him royalties, and make him rich.

"I showed 'em exactly how the body needed to be shaped, and how I made the spoon out of the heavy metal rim around a Model A Ford's headlight," he recalled when I talked with him recently. "But they dawdled around a few years and finally told me a bait like mine would just cost too much to make. Then, after my patents finally ran out, they came out with a bait that sure is shaped like mine. And danged if they didn't name it the 'Model A.' But I doubt that was intentional. Hell, those people I dealt with at Bomber are probably long since gone."

When I moved to Austin in the mid 1940s to attend the University of Texas, I took with me a precious cigar box full of Layfield lures and promptly developed a reputation as some sort of kid prodigy bass fisherman. But it was mostly the lures, which the fish had never seen, and the fact that the chain of Colorado River lakes west of Austin were new, fertile, and full of bass.

Since I had no car, I'd take a city bus to the river, air up my canvas-covered inner-tube floater at a service station, and float-fish down to the next bridge crossing. One cold, wet February day, fishing with my raincoat draped over my inner tube, I was catching a fish nearly every cast. The occupants of a nearby boat, apparently unfamiliar with inner-tube floaters and assuming I was wading, got so excited that the guy in the bow jumped overboard, leaving only his cap floating in about 10 feet of water. His buddy had to crank the outboard to retrieve him from downstream.

In grasshopper time, the feisty native river bass (Guadalupe spotted bass) would go bananas over a yellow Cotton's Topwater bounced off shady undercut banks. And in the late afternoons when the fish came out to feed in swift riffles, Jess' straight swimming plug was the ticket. Largemouths were found mostly in calm sloughs, and were suckers for a pearl-colored skirt bait with its pollywog wiggle. But in early spring, when prespawning largemouths gathered around the mouths of these sloughs, the old original Layfield—allowed to settle almost to the bottom and retrieved as slowly as it would wobble—was almost like cheating.

The most fun of all was walking Cotton's Topwater over the mats of vegetation on Lake Austin, particularly around the mouth of Bee Creek where there was a fine lakefront dance hall, with big bands on the jukebox. My fishing buddy Jake Posey and I would a rent a canoe at Bennet's Boat Dock, paddle across the lake, and spend moonlit nights listening to the music of Glenn Miller. . . and surface-blasting bass. We'd cast into little open holes in the mossbeds, giving the little lures time to turn over and get their scorpionlike tails upright, and then we'd crawl 'em slowly over the weed mats and hold onto our rods.

Unlike today's frog or rat imitation that basically slides over vegetation, this little hummer *walked.* And when bass blew up through the salad, they were definitely trying to kill it. We missed more than we hooked, but we caught some big bass.

Those little lures ultimately gave me my start in the outdoor-writing business. I brought so many stringers of bass back to the boarding-house cook—and to bribe city bus drivers into letting my wet, moss-stinking inner-tube floater aboard—that word got around.

One day when I had a particularly big

bass (just under 8 pounds; in the days before Florida-strain bass were introduced to Texas, that was big) the bus driver stopped and called the Austin newspaper. A photographer was waiting when I changed buses at Sixth Street and Congress Avenue. The picture ran big, and I got my first story assignment from the old *Texas Game, Fish, and Oyster Commission* magazine. I've been selling outdoor stories ever since.

The Layfield lures haven't been so lucky. I tried my best to convince an Austin plastics-molding company to produce them under a royalty arrangement for the Layfields, and it just might have happened had the company not, a few days earlier, signed a contract to produce a locally invented lure—an oversized and awesomely ugly frog that burped water and kicked its legs when jerked. As far as I know, the only belly flop it ever made was financial.

Meanwhile, there were many clones of the original Layfield body shape appearing on the market. Layfield had both the design and mechanical patents, but not the money to protect them in court. Yet he believed his lures were better than any of the others, and that sooner or later some wealthy backer would come along.

What did come along was a part-time preacher with promises of making Layfield rich by setting up an injection-molding plant to produce the lures in high volume. That operation became Sunnybrook Lure Company of Tyler, Texas, which Jess says was over-promised, underfinanced, and underpromoted. At any rate it failed before very many anglers heard of it. Some years later, one of Jess' relatives unsuccessfully tried to market the Skirt Bait, but again without adequate advertising or promotion.

— ✠ —

NOW ALL THE patents on Layfield lures, including Cotton's Topwater, have expired, and anyone can produce them. But I'm told the Topwater and the Skirt Bait would be too expensive to mass-produce, and there are already too many small, wiggling lures similar to the original Layfield shape. (Actually, most of these are diving floaters, whereas the Layfield is a countdown sinker.)

Just the same, lure history has been made, and in some respects the Layfields could be considered the American equivalent of Finland's Rapala family, which also started out whittling lures, but ended up getting rich.

In 1990 I went back to Kerens and looked up the Layfields. Jess was then eighty-two, Cotton eighty-one, both still fishing, and as resourceful as ever. When I needed some lures to photograph, Cotton said he'd look around and see if he had any of the old parts left for his Topwaters.

A couple of months later a small package, smelling strongly of skunk, arrived in the mail.

"I'd of got this to you sooner," said the note inside, "but I was plumb out of black bucktail, and it took a while to find a fresh roadkill."

Cotton died last year. And sometimes when I find myself on some farm pond full of pretty water lilies, I make a few casts with the last little yellow Topwater he ever carved, hoping no bass takes it away from me, fishing for memories.

By Doug Pike

Building the BIGGEST BASS

FISHERIES BIOLOGISTS IN TEXAS WON'T COME RIGHT OUT AND SAY SO, BUT THEY'D LIKE THE NEXT WORLD-RECORD LARGEMOUTH BASS TO BE CAUGHT FROM ONE OF THEIR OWN LAKES. AND AFTER TWO DECADES OF WORK, THEY'RE CLOSE TO REALIZING THE GOAL—THE HOLY GRAIL OF BASS FISHING.

TEXAS HAS BEEN stocking Florida-strain largemouths in its public reservoirs since 1972, and right from the start those superior fish had a measurable impact. Biologists capitalized on increasing numbers of big bass in state reservoirs by "borrowing" them, essential-

ly, through an innovative Texas Parks and Wildlife Department program called Share-Lunker. This beneficial project accepts only live, healthy bass that weigh 13 pounds or more by tempting potential contributors with a free replica mount. Whenever and wherever a qualifying fish is caught, the angler can call a 24-hour hotline to have the bass retrieved by a TPWD staffer.

The fish is then transferred to a state hatchery, where it is examined, treated if necessary, and coaxed to spawn. Once its eggs are collected, the sow again belongs to its original captor, who typically requests that it be released in the lake from which it was caught.

Among other duties, scientists in the nine freshwater hatcheries and research centers around the Lone Star State are charged with producing more and bigger bass for recreational fishermen.

ShareLunker has received about 250 qualifying sows to date.

In November of 1996, the TPWD swung open the doors on its latest bass factory, the Freshwater Fisheries Center at Athens. The most notable resident in that facility's outstanding visitor area, incidentally, is a largemouth bass that has been hand-fed almost daily since its capture. In a matter of months, the bass grew from less than 14 pounds (when caught from Brandy Branch Reservoir) to more than 19 pounds. She is an anomaly, of course, but serves as proof positive that proper nutrition,

quality habitat, and superior genetics can be molded into super-heavyweight fish.

BRAGGING RIGHTS

UNDER THE LONE Star, where legend brags of all things being bigger and better, Georgia's claim to the 22-pound 4-ounce world-record largemouth has been a splinter in bassers' backsides now since 1932. Even more irritating to Texans, California lakes already have produced bass in excess of 20 pounds; in 1991, Castaic Lake coughed up a 22-pounder (recognized as the world's best by the International Game Fish Association) that was but a single, hearty meal from knocking the fuzz off the Peach State's perennial peach. And while Texans watched their fishery skyrocket in the late 1980s and early 1990s, it has fizzled and sputtered since then in the race to topple the world benchmark.

Texas' state-record largemouth bass, caught from Lake Fork in 1992 by Barry St. Clair, weighed a respectable 18.18 pounds. In that fish's wake, though, have come no serious threats to the standard. Although the Share-Lunker program continues to accept an average of two dozen fish each December through April, the fattest entry in recent years weighed a relative puny 15 pounds. Not that 15-pounders are inconsequential, but they could hide in the shadow of any potential world-record bass.

If it was real—and credible skeptics remain—George Perry's 1932 catch from Montgomery Lake was a freak. There is no other plausible explanation for a largemouth bass to have reached such gargantuan proportions at a time when, almost anywhere else in the nation, 10-pounders were considered exceptional. With the introduction of Florida and Cuban subspecies to the predominant North American gene pool and enactment of aggressive trophy management regulations, however, the "average" largemouth bass in this country keeps getting larger.

That was the case in Texas, at least, until its aggressive management program took an unusual turn.

Although the state's ShareLunker program has accepted heavyweight entries from nearly three dozen public impoundments now, the showplace is (and likely will remain) Lake Fork; I'm aware of no other lake in the nation (perhaps the world) that produces double-digit bass with such frequency and consistency. Lately, you can't even get marina owners to snap instant photos of bass that scale less than 10 or 12 pounds; literally hundreds of fish in that

The Freshwater Fisheries Center in Athens, Texas (above and opposite page, top), features an outstanding visitor center where anglers can view live specimens in glass-walled tanks as well as mounts in a display case.

class are caught from this lake each year, and nothing smaller will raise local eyebrows.

To emphasize Lake Fork's importance to Texas bassers and the thousands of visitors who make annual pilgrimages each winter and spring, the sprawling impoundment near Dallas has produced thirty-six of the state's Top 50 bass—all heavier than 15 pounds—as well as every one of the state's six fish that weighed 17 pounds or more, including St. Clair's record-setting catch.

Most of the fish on that roster, regardless of where they were caught, came during that brief boom in the late 1980s. From 1988 through 1991, Top 50 bookkeepers at TPWD reached for their erasers twenty-nine times. Since 1992, though, only eight bass have bumped others from the elite list.

"We think Florida bass have the potential to grow [to world-class proportions] under the right conditions," said Kathy Ramos, manager of the state's Tyler hatchery and ShareLunker coordinator. "The program has been successful in one way, not so successful in another."

On the plus side, fishermen have been educated to the benefits of catch-and-release; if you leave fish out there, they'll get bigger. (Or so the theory goes; more on that later.) Otherwise, there have been problems getting some fish to spawn in captivity.

On the other hand, "We're not able to collect eggs on a consistent basis," Ramos said. "These fish won't spawn if they don't think

Since only one in ten fish has the specific genetics to reach record size, technicians sample DNA from prospective breeders.

they're going to survive. Most of the fish caught (and loaned to ShareLunker) are on average ten years old; it's like asking Grandma to run a marathon, then spawn."

Most significant of all, perhaps, is that scientists have yet to discover any inheritability of exceptional growth.

Since the Athens facility came on line, however, biologists now have the technology and working space to monitor several generations of offspring from a single, superior bass. They're even able to genetically "fingerprint" juvenile largemouths so they can be identified as coming from a particular female no matter when or where or how much later the fish are recaptured.

THE LIMITS OF GROWTH

ACCORDING TO AN independent fisheries expert, however, the same factors that made Lake Fork such an exceptional fishery for 10-pound bass also may be keeping it from producing a 23-pounder. Mac McCune, owner of Lake Management Services in Texas, works with hundreds of landowners to improve the quality of fish in their stock tanks and reservoirs. He believes that catch-and-release actually may be hurting fishermen's chances for bigger bass.

The factors that most greatly influence the growth of a bass are genetics, forage, and the growing season, McCune said, and to a lesser degree, water fertility. With-

out all these elements, a fish cannot reach its maximum potential size.

Using Lake Fork's bass as an example, McCune acknowledged their exceptional genetics, a long growing season, and good fertility "There's only one other factor, and that's the forage base," he said. "If you don't have size diversity in the forage base, bass growth stops relative to the forage size."

Fork went through years of phenomenal bass growth, which put tremendous pressure on its forage base. And since fishermen there have adopted a self-imposed release rule on big bass, McCune proposes, the lake's forage species haven't been able to keep pace.

"If there aren't enough bass taken out of a lake," he said, "forage can't satisfy the demand. There's a lot of speculation, but that's the theory—whether you're talking about 10 acres of water or 10,000 acres."

On a smaller scale, for example, imagine a stock pond primed with 100 Florida bass, each weighing about 1 pound. Assume good fertility and a healthy population of adult bluebills to produce forage. Through their first few years, the young largemouths gorge themselves on juvenile panfish. The landowner and his buddies fish regularly, but they release every bass they catch. A season or two later, the bass weigh 3 or 4 pounds each, and they're consuming all the young bluegills that the pond can produce.

The next spring, those same bass are crowding 5 and 6 pounds. Fishing's great, and the

Hatchery workers constantly monitor the weight and size of fish in the big bass program.

landowner can't wait until his bass are all 10-pounders.

Those 6-pounders (and their offspring), though, go through the pond's little bluegills quickly. The lake's biggest bass—which require larger prey to continue growing—turn on the pond's adult forage fish. As the number of breeding-class bluegills is reduced, the pond's forage base begins to collapse. In response, the largemouths essentially go on a diet, and growth stops.

The pond always seems to have plenty of 5- and 6-pound fish but nothing any larger. Lake Fork, because its anglers are so quick to release their trophy bass, may be in the middle of just such a cycle.

"If recreational pressure hasn't declined," McCune said, "you have to assume that the [super-heavyweight] fish simply aren't there."

In other words, catch-and-release may have made Lake Fork the nation's premier producer of 10- and 12-pound bass and even a few 17-pounders, but it also may be the reason that the lake has yet to cough up a 20-pounder.

"We're reevaluating some of the stocking programs," said Roger McCabe, from Texas' Waco hatchery, "and looking at managing some lakes as truly trophy lakes."

BUILT-TO-ORDER BASS

ALREADY, SAID TPWD's Director of Inland Fisheries Phil Durocher, state hatcheries are being revamped to perform specific tasks. Some will focus on producing high quantities of bass tough enough to handle wide temperature and fertility fluctuations; others will concentrate strictly on trophy-class fish. Texas anglers want both, and the state is in a unique position now to accommodate them.

Durocher said that throughout his hatch-

...the bass to beat all bass, the largemouth that will rewrite the record book.

ery system, strict attention is paid to diversity; the state's brood fish are replaced every five years to eliminate potential for defects caused by inbreeding. Diversity is especially critical, he said, for producing bass with the potential to reach exceptional length and weight.

"Maybe only one in ten, one in 100 fish get those specific genetics [to reach record size]," Durocher said. "We've got to be able to identify them."

According to McCune, those fish aren't so hard to pick from a lineup.

"Once a bass hits 10 pounds," McCune said, "the genetics are there to grow bigger. If a bass hits 12 pounds and has enough forage, it should be able to get to 15 or 16 pounds."

Or, theoretically, 23 pounds.

The new Athens facility is state-of-the-art, and Texas' other hatcheries are hardly antiques. They'll keep cranking out "good" bass to satisfy recreational fishing needs, but researchers are every bit as keen on developing the bass to beat all bass, the largemouth that will rewrite the record book.

"We don't look at it as a competition [between states]," McCabe said, "but..."

"I think we're ahead of the other states," Ramos said. "A lot of agencies are asking us questions."

Durocher is confident that the Texas largemouth bass program has no equal, and he's just as sure that his staff can produce a world-record largemouth bass. Department-wide optimism has increased, too, with the debut of that fast-growing showpiece at Athens.

"She's a ham; she likes to come right up to the glass," Durocher said. "If there's something special about that fish, we'd like to pass that on."

And so the scientists continue to study their notes, ponder what is yet the impossible, coddle extraordinary fish, and wait.

By Ken Schultz

In Search of a
10-POUND BASS

ANGLING IS ALWAYS AN UNCERTAINTY—ESPECIALLY FOR BIG FISH—BUT THESE WATERS WILL BETTER THE ODDS FOR YOU.

That's it! The buzzer sounds, the audience screams, and we win the grand prize: a trip to the destination of our choice to fish for 10-pound bass.

So, where to? Florida, Texas, Mexico, and California immediately come to mind.

A recent study of trophy largemouths in Florida showed that one-third of the fish weighing more than 10 pounds came from waters measuring 500 acres or less. Biologists say it's because such waters often receive less attention. Small waters are sometimes tricky to find but if you ask folks to point you toward a pond or small lake that isn't heavily fished, you might be rewarded with a 10.

Among the state's big waters, Lake Okeechobee is a leading candidate for producing 10-pounders. Although the lake suffered from

WE'RE PLAYING Password and seconds remain for me to guess the last topic from a series of your one-word clues.

You say, "Ten." I say, "Bo Derek."
You say, "Pounds." I say, "Scale."
You say, "Fish." I say, "Bass."

low-water drought conditions and winds in recent years, the abundance of rain in 1992 may have primed Okeechobee for one of its best seasons in a long time. The seemingly endless growing season, fertile water, and warm temperatures contribute to an average growth rate of 1.3 pounds per year, making for lots of big bass.

Okeechobee, with 730 square miles of water and 200,000-odd surface acres, is practically an inland ocean. However, it's so shallow in most places that you can stick your rod into the water and touch bottom without even getting your hand wet. Although bass are always accessible, the mile upon mile of grassy flats and rim canals pose the difficult question of where to fish, especially for a trophy. Without a guide, a newcomer could be in for a lot of prospecting before hitting pay dirt.

Nevertheless, the Big O offers a distinct advantage. Located in southcentral Florida atop the Everglades, it is the state's least-affected big-bass water during late winter and early spring. Florida bass are notorious for shutting down after a cold front, but south Florida simply doesn't get as cold as the rest of the state, nor is it as frequently affected by northerly fronts. Thus, the angling is more stable, and the bass more active.

A relatively stable water, located in northeastern Florida, which is also primed for good fishing, is Rodman Reservoir on the Oklawaha River. Known to most as Rodman Pool, it can be reached from the famous St. Johns River, via a lock that helps control water levels and allows the passage of watercraft up the Oklawaha through Silver Springs.

The current average size of fish in Rodman is large (in a major tournament last February the average weight of over two dozen bass caught was nearly 3 pounds each), and the potential for a trophy is encouraging.

Outside of Florida, exports of the Florida-strain bass have taken hold in a number of lakes, especially in Mexico, Texas, and California.

Mexico, which was once synonymous with arm-tiring loads of small bass, now boasts three thriving big-bass lakes—Guerrero, Baccarac, and Comedero. Lake Guerrero may provide the best chance for a bass over 10 pounds, but you'll have to be satisfied with a low overall catch and the fact that perhaps only one in ten visiting anglers will have a chance at such a fish.

Although it's a large impoundment, Guerrero is about 25 feet below normal levels at the moment, up from a 50-foot low due to half a decade of drought. Despite the toll this has taken on the overall fish population, continued recovery, along with bigger bass, is imminent. Now the brushy reservoir is producing 10- to 15-pound fish, and even a reported 17-pounder.

Baccarac, on the other hand, has produced three fish in the 16-pound class and is likely to have more like that, as well as 10-pounders. Baccarac first opened for fishing in 1983, so it is still a young fishery, and the Floridas are obviously taking hold.

Lake Comedero, originally named Lake José Lopez Portillo, was formed in 1981 and opened in 1986, when it was stocked then with

Saving That Trophy

One of the reasons why it's difficult to catch big bass is because of intense angling pressure and the fact that many big bass which are caught are kept. Clearly there is a need for anglers in heavily and moderately fished waters to release big fish. And in this era of high-quality replica taxidermy mounts, there is no need to keep the actual fish.

Be prepared by having all of the necessary equipment close at hand before you hook your trophy. By handling your catch carefully—with wet hands so as not to hurt the scales—you can take a quick photograph and measure the length and girth so you can have the fish replicated.

Carefully resuscitating the bass and returning it to the water quickly will aid its release and recovery. The release will contribute to the gene pool and possibly provide another angler—maybe you or your children—with future enjoyment.—K.S.

fingerling Florida bass. It produced several largemouths in the 7- to 10-pound range each year. The difference between Comedero and the other lakes, besides age, is that Comedero is producing lots of fish, with the average size being close to 4 pounds, offering the best bet for the combination of size and action.

The problem with fishing in Mexico is that bass are not a gamefish, and can be freely netted. Big largemouths are often kept by locals, as well as sport fishermen, and this may mean that the fishery will become mediocre in time. However, Dan Snow's Bass Tours, one of the three camps at Lake Comedero, promotes catch-and-release fishing. In fact, the company offers a 10 percent rebate to anglers who release their fish there as well as at other Mexican lakes.

———— ✦≣✦≣✦ ————

FLORIDA FISH ARE being caught and released in trophy proportions in Texas' Lake Fork, a 27,000-acre impoundment that could well offer the best chance of catching a bass of 10 pounds or better in American waters. In fact, it probably offers the best chance of getting one over 12 pounds. In January of 1992, the state and lake record was broken by an 18.18-pounder. Lake Fork has produced sixteen of the top twenty bass caught in Texas, and some feel that a world record is lurking in its depths.

Impounded in 1980, Lake Fork is filled with plenty of timber and a good forage base of shad; a slot limit helps regulate the growth of its Florida-strain largemouths. The really large fish are not necessarily easy to catch, but bass of 10-pounds-plus have been taken at all times of the season.

Texas has one of the nation's most aggressive bass management systems, and is especially focusing on quality fishing with the introduction of Florida-strain bass into various state waters. As a matter of fact, a new high-tech fish hatchery is operating in San Marcos, producing Florida fingerlings for stocking.

One of the waters receiving these fish is Lake Sam Rayburn, a mammoth East Texas lake that has been through boom-bust times. A drought and drawdown over a decade ago has helped spur the growth of new cover, including vegetation such as buck brush, willows, and hydrilla. Bass are prospering, growing quickly, and attaining a large average size in this rich 45-mile-long reservoir.

But discovering which submerged creek channels, back bays, flats, and dropoffs have the best cover to produce the bigger bass takes some doing on this 114,000-acre water, with its 560 miles of shore. The services of a guide are recommended for the first-timer. The lake record is 12 pounds 4 ounces, small by modern Texas standards, but the Floridas that were stocked here in the late 1980s are in the 10-pound plus class now, so watch out.

A lot of eyes, and anglers, are also looking to Castaic Lake in Southern California, where three fish over 20 pounds nearly toppled the sixty-year-old world record for bass in 1991. This is an extremely popular lake, and the average angler must work hard to catch a bass over 10 pounds.

Most of Castaic's lunkers are taken with precise fishing techniques, using light line and live bait. Created in 1971, Castaic is a bare-banked, coverless, canyon-like impoundment of only 2,500 acres. Heavy fishing pressure is the rule, and the bass, especially the bigger ones, which are the product of Florida-strain stockings, are tough to come by.

Of course, big bass do not come easy anywhere, although the odds are better in some places than others. Whether you catch a 10-pounder or not, don't underestimate the excitement and the intensity of fishing at one of these waters—where any cast *could* produce the trophy of a lifetime.

By W. Hardbark McLoughlin

Looking
BASSACKWARDS

IT TOOK AN APPARITION FROM PREHISTORY TO REVEAL THE ANCIENT ORIGINS OF OUR MOST SOPHISTICATED SPORT.

TWO YEARS AGO THIS writer set the scientific world on its ear by succeeding in a quest that had cost lesser men their fortunes, their reputations, and yes, even their sanity. In a dark, fishbone-littered grotto, its limestone walls adorned with angling frescoes unseen by human eyes for ten thousand years, I found the world's oldest bass boat. It was an archaeological event equalled only by the unearthing of Tutankhamen's tomb.

My quest had its origin with my reading of *Just for the Hull of It—The Search for the Original Bassboat,* by the "Anglin' Anthropologist," Orlando Mead.* As an ardent arkeologist (one who studies old boats) I was mesmerized; I felt the hardships and disappointments of the author's search through his vivid, heart-wrenching description of his quest and its ultimate failure.

While in the midst of my reading, a ghostly figure appeared, naked but for a scrap of fur about his waist. His unusually long arms held a primitive tackle box and a bait-casting rod spooled with 20-pound-test sinew. The apparition's deep-set eyes stared into my soul, and its voice told me: "It is up to YOU! March on where others have fallen." In that moment, I accepted the call of destiny.

Mead's search had centered on an immense labyrinth in a part of the ancient world that was a center of bass worship. Certain that the answer lay in that labyrinth, I pored for weeks over the thousands of photos in Professor Mead's book, using a jeweler's loupe to ferret out the tiniest details.

Nine weeks into my quest, in a photo on page 2316, I saw something extraordinary which convinced me that the boat existed. Barely visible above the spot where the hysterical Orlando beat his head on the cavern wall, was a pictograph which equated a large bass with a hog!

Three days later I was there—Laskoal Cave in Flippin, Arkansas. In no time I found the vessel, the cause of so much human tragedy, not 100 feet from the place where Orlando's brain had suffered its final backlash.

With tears streaming down my face, I marveled at how little bassboat design had changed since that glorious birchbark craft was built. Who could have guessed that pedestal seats were that old, and that even then, the front seat was the best? I gazed in awe upon the granite anchors, the simple knotted sinew line that served as depth finder, the short-paddle "trolling motor." There was even a livewell that was aerated by blowing through a reed. It was overwhelming!

What unknown genius devised the crude wooden drivetrain lashed to the transom? I imagined our fishing forefathers furiously cranking themselves across a lake to their favorite honey hole. My heart tightened, thinking of a loin-clothed craftsman using only a sliver of flint the size of a potato chip to carve a weedless prop from a 14-pound chunk of hickory. When I read the pictograph on the boat's side proclaiming, "I... BASS... MAN!" I knew I had to share this mystical experience with my fellow man.

With a $700,000 grant from B.A.R.G. (Bassin' Antiques Restoration Group) and matching Federal funds, I set about preserving the priceless craft for future generations.

Since the dried-out bark hull was too fragile, I scrapped it, replacing it with a glass Bassin' Banshee hull from Screamer Marine. Since the new hull is magenta, I had new color-coordinated fully adjustable pedestal seats installed. They're servo-controlled, and the front one has a lumbar massage unit.

Since I want to be cranking a reel and not some maple motor, I hung a 175-horsepower River Eater XJ from Firestorm Racing on the stern. It's loud, but I can still hear my tunes thanks to Sound Barrier's incredible thirty-speaker system, which has the moxie to create chop 10 feet from the boat.

The original running torches would never stay lit at 85 mph, so I dumped them for Super Nova halogens complete with a pair of 1,250,000-candlepower spots. You can bet *I'll* find the ramp after sunset! The knotted strings didn't look right, so now there are seventeen screens telling where I am, what I'm over, and what the temperature and pH of all of it is.

The new livewell is as big as a wading pool, temperature-controlled, and its ForceFive aerator could inflate a blimp. The whole rig's cradled down the blacktop by a fluid-suspension Hull Hugger Demon from Nemo Trailer. I got the matching bus, too. It says "I... BASS... MAN!" right on the side.

We'll be at all the major tourneys this year, so stop by. You can meet me and my driver Orlando. See ya there!

⊷ ⋈ ⊶

*SON OF ANTHROPOLOGIST Mavis Mead, namesake of Lake Mead, the 3-acre New Jersey salt flat where tool manufacturers test bubble levels.

By Ken Schultz

The Strange Story of the Record
LARGEMOUTH BASS

SOMEONE MAY
CATCH A BIGGER
BASS, BUT THE
LEGENDARY
STATUS OF
GEORGE PERRY'S
FISH WON'T BE
SURPASSED.

SOUTH GEORGIA'S ROADS
have many long straightaways
that are conducive to speeding and daydreaming.
They are flanked by tall pines, fields of cotton, peanuts,

without permission by a freelance writer and never returned.

→•—·★◆★·—•←

GEORGE PERRY BECAME an industrious self-made man, one who reportedly was liked by almost everyone. He worked in a shipyard in World War II, ran a marina for a while, was once the manager of the Brunswick, Georgia, airport, repaired airplanes, and became a pilot. He owned many planes and became the busy owner of a flying service in Brunswick.

He reportedly cared little about the fact that he had caught the record bass, and was both astounded and amused by the interest in the fish in later years. He caught a FIELD & STREAM contest-winning 13-pound 4-ounce bass in 1934, and fished occasionally through the years, especially in the Altamaha River and in saltwater. He was apparently contacted a lot by fishermen, and told his story to various journalists over the years. He told Terry Drace that he got a Pflueger Supreme reel for a statement he made for that company, but received nothing else for the catch other than the first-prize merchandise.

George Perry died in 1974 when a plane he was piloting crashed into a mountainside in thick fog at the Birmingham, Alabama, airport.

Montgomery Lake still exists, despite some reports to the contrary, but it is not much of a lake, and has changed a good deal in sixty years. Many people in Telfair County as well as the rest of south Georgia don't know where it is, or don't realize that Montgomery Lake is not really a lake, but an oxbow of the Ocmulgee River. Many who see it are disappointed.

When I saw it last fall, Montgomery Lake was stagnant and pea soup colored, looking mostly like an alligator hole. The lake still has largemouth bass, which are called trout or green trout by many south Georgians, but it is not known as a bass lake locally. Those few who fish it usually are looking for bream. A faded wooden sign at the lake commemorates Perry's catch.

Ronnie Walker, an avid angler and the sheriff of Telfair County, is proud of Perry's bass and its meaning to Georgia (which made the largemouth bass its state fish, primarily because of the record) and to Telfair County. He sums up the feeling of some local folks, who are aware that their native son's record may be broken soon by a California fish which will be worth mega dollars to the angler who

The Lure That Caught the Record

Much ado has been made about the No. 2401 Creek Chub Wiggle Fish that has repeatedly been credited with catching George Perry's record bass. The Wiggle Fish was the 2400 series of Creek Chub lures. It was a jointed minnow-imitation wooden plug with a metal lip blade, two treble hooks, two line-tie positions, and a fluted nickel tail that wagged when the lure was retrieved.

According to the 1932 FIELD & STREAM fishing contest results, however, which were published in the April 1933 issue of that magazine, the lure that caught Perry's fish was a "Creek Chub No 2103." Carl Luckey, in his book *Old Fishing Lures and Tackle*, identifies the 2100 series lure as being the Fin Tail Shiner. It was also wooden but not jointed, and sported a metal lip blade, two treble

hooks, two line-tie positions, and either flexible or metal fins.

This is the description of the Fin Tail Shiner in Luckey's book: "New in 1924, this lure underwent a few significant changes before it was eliminated from the catalogs by 1944. First available [with] flexible fiber dorsal and tail fins. About 1930 another flexible fiber fin was added to each side of the head just under the eyes. The 1938 catalog is the first time the lure description mentioned metal fins although they used the same cut as the older models to illustrate the lure. It said '...Swishing metal fins.'"

Whichever lure it was, it seems that the color that caught the record was a natural perch finish or pattern. Both lures were made in a (yellow) perch finish.

AMERICA'S FISH

catches it. Said Walker, "I'd rather not see the record broken, but if it is, [it should] be broken by someone like George Perry, not someone who makes his living from the sport or fishes every day."

There are a lot of people, primarily in California, hunting hard for the next world-record largemouth bass. Times have changed, circumstances are different, the interest in such a fish is high, and the next record will probably make its captor feel like a lottery winner. With two 20-pounders having been caught at Castaic Lake, California, in 1991, including a 22.01-pound fish that was landed and admirably released by Bob Crupi (that fish had a 29½-inch length and 27½-inch girth, incidentally), the odds favor a new record coming from there.

There is some irony in comparing then and now in terms of the attention paid to largemouth bass and records, the tackle and boats used, the rewards to be reaped, and the kinds of waters and genetics involved. The latter subject is an especially compelling one, for the bass in California are transplants from Florida-strain largemouth bass and are not a natural inhabitant of their waters.

Does it matter? George Perry was asked about the huge California bass by Terry Drace in 1974. He said, ". . . A record bass, or a record anything, should be taken in its natural state. With all this replanting and crossbreeding, you can produce almost anything you want. Only Nature should be allowed to produce anything for a record. In my opinion, these Super Bass never will compare to the bass I caught in Montgomery Lake. I certainly think if a record bass is caught, it should be caught in the natural waters of its habitation, on a hook and line."

Perry also had some thoughts about the state of bass fishing in 1974, which he would no doubt still harbor today. "Everything has changed so," he told Drace. "I had a little ol' 14-foot boat that probably cost me 30 cents worth of material and built my first one myself. We've come a long way from the 59-cent rod and 19-cent line I had years ago to the $5,000 worth of equipment now to go fishing. I guess bass fishing has come a long way, though sometimes I wonder."

Editor's note: The author wishes to express thanks to Ken Holyoak, Malcolm Vernadoe, Ronnie Walker, Bill Baab, and Peter Ryals for their assistance.

By Joe Doggett

YESTERDAY'S BASS

TIRED OF FISHING IN THE FAST LANE? LOOK WHAT HAPPENS WHEN YOU STEP BACK AND SLOW DOWN.

THE ROD AND REEL were from a forgotten place. The last time the split cane and simple gears were considered functional, Sam Rayburn was the Speaker of the House, not the namesake of the lake, and Elvis Presley drove a truck.

But the tackle was more than a curiosity; it was a reminder.

Bass fishing has changed. The focus has moved from the backwaters to the big top and, in doing so, the circus has become increasingly second class. Not the anglers, the best of whom are masters, and not the equipment, the finest of which is excellent, but the experience.

We've lost something. During the transition from bamboo to graphite, from dripping paddles to roaring roostertails, the typical bass fishing trip has been downgraded from exceptional to routine. "Routine" usually consists of chunk-and-wind casting with subsurface crankbaits, or bumping bottom with weighted plastics.

These patterns of covering open water and probing deep structure are endorsed by most professionals and many amateurs. To the pro, the guide, or tournament angler, time is money; these experts are concerned with the most efficient ways of locating and catching bass. To the beginner, a bass by any means is a big deal, and crankbaits and worms are proven routes to success. In either boat, aesthetics rate a distant second to weigh-in.

This run-and-gun fishing is legitimate and effective—and boring. I suppose I would rather snatch deep school bass on worms and crankbaits than listen to select readings from obscure Middle English poets, but the vibrant kick is missing. Again, I do not mean to belittle the skills and talents necessary to stay on fish, but how many 1- and 2-pound bass can you catch from monotone water before you start losing the edge, the stoke, that put you there? This is not what made bass fishing great. What happened to the main-line contact and the big hit?

The answer might wait in the patient old tackle. A 1992 statistic revealed that the average bass angler is a forty-year-old male; in other words, today's typical angler grew his bald spot over plastic and graphite and three-digit horsepower. The equipment I cleaned and readied is unknown to him. So, perhaps, is its philosophy.

The outdated gear was designed to fish slow and close and shallow, not fast and random and deep. It was ineffective in the fast

lane, not that much of a speed track existed in the years predating large reservoirs and high-tech boats. The rod was a 5½-foot bamboo Heddon Reliable, a utility grade with a stiff action and short, straight cork grip. The only affectation was a curved metal trigger guard. The blank carried five small, silk-wrapped guides and the slight bend, or "set," that is the enduring and honorable signature of cane under use. The chrome Shakespeare Criterion was a direct—make that direct-drive—descendant of the Kentucky reels. Yes, an antique B.F. Meeks & Sons No. 2, or maybe a B.C. Milam No. 3 would have been more authentic, but, well, I didn't have one. But, the Criterion with its trim, round side plates and hopelessly small grips was true to its origin and beautiful in simplicity—no squatty, space-age profile, no thumb bar, no anti-backlash magnets, no flipping lever, no disengaging level wind, no adjustable internal drag, no. . . bells and whistles.

The soft patina of polished metal and aged cane glowed with purpose. The tackle was antique in the angling sense, but it felt good. It was balanced. Functional. A thread—not of monofilament but of braided Dacron—connected past and present, not to mention a wooden surface plug. We went bass fishing.

———— ✦✦✦ ————

"DAMN!" I MUTTERED, thumbing against a whirring backlash and watching the red-and white Heddon Basser sail and stutter awry. Timing and reflexes tuned to freespooling were out of synch with the tempo of fifty years ago. But the venue was not.

I was working a johnboat along the bank of a 500-acre river-bottom lake. The black-clear water was rich with weeds and brush and logs. Frogs croaked and peeped against the gathering afternoon. A bulbous alligator snout disappeared with a hiss of bubbles and stately flights of egrets and ibises coasted overhead. Redwing blackbirds bounced through shoreline stalks. It was classic bass water and there was no contest in sight.

This was the core of bait-casting. The spool whirred and the small handle grips blurred and you thumbed the outrushing momentum—and the devil take mechanical backlash controls. The introduction remained awkward. I picked at another minor snarl and rewound, holding the incoming line between thumb and forefinger as the dainty level wind fed the spool.

The braided line tested 12 pounds, borderline heavy but the lightest I could find (fly reel backing, actually; try to locate a spool of Ashaway or Old Cronie bait-casting line on today's shelves). The old pluggers, the gents with weathered faces and knuckly hands who wore Panama hats and white shirts buttoned at the neck, preferred 9- and 10-pound lines for smooth casting.

The rig worked better once the line was wet. You learn these things. I aimed at an outpost of reeds. The rod loaded against the no-nonsense heft of the 5/8-ounce payload but the Basser fell about 5 feet from the reeds. Not good. The old pluggers deplored sloppy casting. I am right-handed and the slow-starting delivery had a tendency to torque to the left. With a bit of compensation and a measure of appropriate "Kentucky windage," the tackle and I achieved a workable compromise.

The lack of anti-reverse capability was a recurring embarrassment during the idle moments between casts. Each time the thumb wandered from the spool the weight of the unrestrained and dangling plug caused the reel handle to backspin. Not only would the unmonitored spool snarl, the plug would drop several feet from its correct and loaded position below the rod tip. Unsuspecting of any mutiny, I would turn to face a prime target and scramble out of control. A life of anti-reverse is a hard habit to break.

Authority and expertise grew as the boat eased down the shoreline. The gear was down-right capable, especially at the closer ranges in which the rules of engagement were defined. The tackle was not intended for chunking far across open water or for probing deep trenches. You work close, aim at a visible target, and lay it in tight and right the first time. Each cast

Each cast was a precise decision, not a blind hope.

was a precise decision, not a blind hope. This is the traditional creed of bait-casting for bass.

The little reel made a pleasant purring as the handle spun with the cast. Put a drop of oil on the pawl, a confident wrist behind the effort, and you could feel the bamboo spring to life. The Basser's gaudy flight was smooth and accurate—well, maybe occasionally drifting to the left. A low side-arm could punch the plug into the wind. The limp line was remarkably tolerant. Monofilament with its nagging coiled "memory" tends to boil under the least mistake, especially when directed upwind, but the wetted braid was slow to incite to riot. I am not claiming that the rig was superior to contemporary tackle, but it was real. A lot of today's young lions would be surprised at how well it fished.

The rod and reel felt comfortable as I methodically plugged the secluded and shadowed shallows. Here, we had returned to level-wind roots. The mood would have been out of place in a big, loud boat on a big, loud lake, backed by aggressive tactics and electronic assault equipment.

THE STUDIED PACE was not an illusion; the wobbling plunk and gurgle of the old plug was most effective with a seductive crawl. Not that you have much choice. The retrieve ratio of the old reel is about 3-to-1, compared to the 5-to-1 and 6-to-1 rippers fashionable today for covering water. The woefully slow Criterion forced me to decelerate from the pace that normally grips my fishing. Once I quit fighting the rush, the reel seemed well designed for coaxing through the cattails and coontail.

At one point, suffering a bad case of the quaints, I replaced the floating/diving lure with an ancient subsurface plug fitted with twirling propellers and sprouting trebles. I took special care to cinch the soft braid tight. Following a few nervous presentations, I returned to the Basser. The Dowagiac Minnow, as a collectible, was worth more than $100—expensive fodder for the inevitable snag. Besides, the sinking plug did not feel right; it was blind ambition, the origin of the crankbait attitude. The magic was missing unless the retrieve was within swirling distance of the top.

The Basser was talking trash, plopping and chuggling and jiving, and the afternoon was looking better. The air was cooler, the shadows longer, the weeds darker. The plug landed in a wind-riffled pocket. The offering bobbled and fluttered—and a bass struck. This was a real fish, a headhunter. It hit with a powerful boil and a bold, thick turn. I gripped the handle and lifted the rod and felt the weight of the fish. The contact was immediate, the result of the stiff tip and the non-stretch line. You don't realize how spongy elastic mono feels, especially against distance and depth. I came tight to the fight and the hooks were set, deft and sure. It was positive sensation. The fish leaped, shaking with open gills and waggling the Basser, then fell back and dug for the logs. I thumbed the run. The handle spun in reverse as the spool turned under the insistent thumb. The direct contact was a thrilling contrast to the sterile efficiency of a pre-set star drag. I could feel the urgency and strength of the fish.

The bass went deep and found weeds. I levered the rod, favoring the light line, and extracted the impacted fish. It glided to the surface, mired in coontail, a beautiful bass that glistened and bristled in the low light. It would weigh perhaps 5 pounds but measured significantly more at the moment.

The heavy old plug plucked cleanly from the lip as I slipped the fish into the water. The rough jaw had stitched a fine trace in the enamel, proud new scratches to blend with those of decades past. I forgot to clamp the spool or engage the clicker and the lure unraveled to the deck and backlashed the reel. During the last hour of light I landed and released two smaller bass then missed a violent finale. The unseen lunker rose against the gathering dusk and turned a dark and mighty swirl around the wavering plug. The weight ticked through the line but the fish missed the hooks. All nine of them. Jeez. Six pounds? Eight?

The opportunity was lost, reclaimed by fading ripples, but the statement was forged. That big bass and that old tackle were clean, without pretense. They didn't give a damn about decals and digital scales, and the contact was no meek tap or random rap. The terrible and sudden blast carried all the cruelty and elegance of the swamp. This was yesterday's bass.

Bass Through the Seasons

Bass don't migrate like waterfowl or mourning doves, but that doesn't mean they stay put. They frequently relocate, according to the changing nature of their world. When forage fish move into a newly flooded flat, the bass are often right behind. And in the dog days of summer, bass seek the cooler more comfortable water found in the deeper sections of a lake.

What does this mean to you? It means you need to adapt to changing conditions. Yesterday's bass may have moved on, and you need to know where they have gone. If knowledge is power (and it is), your power comes from a thorough understanding of how seasonal change affects bass behavior.

Seasonal change is a multilayered phenomenon. The transition from spring to fall is a far-reaching shift noticeable to any angler, but the more subtle transition of, say, a falling barometer, may go unnoticed. Though the articles in this section may not turn you into a meteorologist or even a bass biologist, at least you'll understand how and why bass move—all of which helps ensure that you'll be able to find fish when they get in a wandering mood.

SINCE 1895

FIELD & STREAM

THE SOUL OF THE AMERICAN OUTDOORS

By Mark Hicks

BASS
on the Move

WHEN FISH GET THE
URGE TO ROAM, YOU'D
BETTER KNOW WHERE
THEY'RE HEADED.

NOTHING CONFUSES anglers more than bass that won't stay put. One day you make an excellent catch from a given structure and the next day the fish have disappeared. Keeping up with vagabond bass is not an exact science, but largemouths are creatures of habit and this can help you determine their next move.

Early in the spring, spawning urges draw bass closer to shallow bedding areas. Likely places are steep creek channel banks, secondary points in creek arms, small points and pockets near deep water, and submerged weedbeds near spawning flats. Slow retrieves with spinnerbaits, crankbaits, and jigs tipped with pork trailers work well during this cold-water period.

Eventually bass move up into their spawning habitat, which is primarily shallow, stable water that receives ample sunlight and offers cover such as weeds, wood, bushes, docks, and rocks. The move to shallow water may be a gradual migration or a sudden rush that seems to occur overnight. When the surface water temperature in the shallows stabilizes at 55 degrees or above on most lakes and reservoirs, many bass make tracks for thin water.

However, spring weather often brings forth sudden squalls and recurring cold fronts that play havoc with bass movements. Torrential rainfalls can raise the water level of impoundments above their normal pool levels, flooding previously dry land.

Bass will move right up with the water into newly flooded bushes, forests, grassy fields, picnic areas, and other man-made structures. Although some fish travel so far back into the trees that you can't reach them by boat, most are within reach of spinnerbaits and crankbaits. Keep on the move and cover the water quickly and don't hesitate to cast to picnic tables, dog houses, and other flooded objects that are not normal bass covers.

As high water subsides, the bass move into more accessible areas, but falling water general-

Bass feeding in submerged weeds readily strike spinnerbaits, lipless rattlers, and diving crankbaits.

ly puts them in a nonbiting mood. So now is a good time to slow down and fish plastic worms and jigs tight to flooded bushes or whatever other cover is available.

Cold fronts are most detrimental in the spring, because a severe northern blast can drive bass right out of the shallows. But don't be too quick to assume the bass have departed. Always keep in mind that shallow bass in good cover are the least likely to move.

After a cold front passes, shallow bass head deep into cover, become sluggish, and usually won't chase fast-moving lures. (Heavy fishing pressure can also make bass respond in this manner.) Anglers who use flipping rods to delicately drop plastic worms and jigs into thick cover can consistently pluck these temperamental bass from their lairs.

Several factors motivate bass movements after the spawn—the most important being food. Bass also are influenced by water temperature, pH levels, availability of cover, and a host of other things, but they'll readily put up with less than desirable conditions to stay near a food source.

I once boated several largemouths in 2 feet of water under a blistering sun that had driven the air temperature to 107 degrees (the surface water temperature was 100 degrees). Why were the bass there? Because the shad were—and the bass were taking advantage of easy and plentiful prey.

Deeper water normally provides bass with more stable conditions. Prime summertime haunts are long, sloping points, humps, and creek channels that afford bass access to both

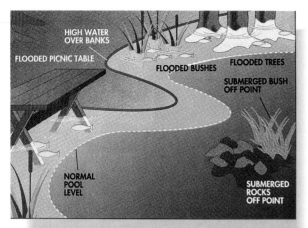
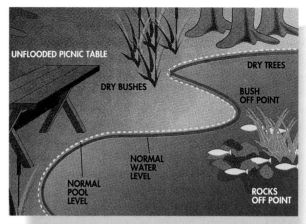

When water rises above the banks, flooding previously dry land, bass move up, occupy the new cover, and feed aggressively (left). As the water recedes (right), the bass leave and use the nearest cover in deeper water, where they'll be more accessible, but less aggressive.

shallow and deep water. Submerged weedbeds, stump rows, flooded trees, rockpiles, or planted brush are consistent producers. Structure with little cover may be loaded with bass one day, but desolate for weeks thereafter.

Bass that have moved off a structure may suspend or follow schools of shad in open water. These fish are extremely difficult to catch; you're better off determining the depth the baitfish and bass are using and checking various structures at that depth. A sonar, particularly a paper or liquid crystal graph with a high-resolution display, is invaluable. It will clearly show suspended baitfish and larger fish in open water and you can determine a depth preference by noting how deep these fish are holding.

Sensitive sonars also show the thermocline, which looks like a cluttered band on the graph. This is caused by plankton and baitfish that have been drawn to the thermocline's cooler, more highly oxygenated water.

Idle over various structures and look for dropoffs and covers that coincide with the preferred depth range. You don't always see bass with sonar devices, so don't hesitate to fish something if it looks particularly inviting.

Deep-diving crankbaits and plastic worms rigged Texas- and Carolina-style are the basic tools for keeping up with summertime bass in deeper structures.

Actively feeding bass in submerged weeds readily strike spinnerbaits, lipless rattlers, and diving crankbaits retrieved right over the top of the vegetation. After a cold front, however, the bass normally drop down into holes in the weeds and often congregate inside weedbeds. They are reluctant biters at this time, but you can coax strikes by slowly fishing plastic worms and jigs.

Submerged structures are productive in the fall, but many bass in impoundments follow shad that migrate up into creek arms and feeder creeks. The bass ambush shad from whatever cover is available—typically visible snags, windfalls, and stumps—and they're usually aggressive enough to belt spinnerbaits and crankbaits. When they're in a more reluctant mood, jigs with pork or plastic trailers are a good bet.

While cold fronts tend to turn bass off in other seasons, they sometimes have just the opposite effect in the fall, especially after the turnover when the bass have become acclimated to cool water. This is the time to don a snowmobile suit, fingerless gloves, and keep slinging. Even when the air temperature plunges into the 30s after a severe front, the bass may be slamming spinnerbaits retrieved next to shallow cover.

Even the best anglers are frequently stumped when bass get the urge to ramble. But the more you know about the seasonal movements of bass and how they respond to changing weather and water conditions, the better you will become at keeping up with vagabond bass.

By Bill Volkart

CHANNEL BASS

WHEN LARGEMOUTHS
DIVE TO RETREAT FROM
THE HEAT, IT PAYS TO
KNOW THE HOTTEST
CHANNEL STRUCTURES.

WHEN THE WATER temperature of a lake nears 80 degrees, many bass move to deep water channels to escape the heat. This may not be news to anyone familiar with hot-weather bass fishing, but the tactics that pay off in the channels might surprise you.

The channels I'm referring to are merely the remains of old streams that once flowed through the area before the lake was impounded. Some will be obvious, and others will be barely noticeable on your depthfinder, but both can produce big bass.

Among the best and easiest spots to find are the points where the old streambed bends sharply. Before impoundment, the outside edge of the bend told the brunt of the stream's current, undercutting the bank and gouging deep holes in the bottom, while the opposite bank remained gently sloped. Bass rest under the old undercut bank and use the spot as an ambush point. And when the channel runs close to the present shoreline, it also offers the bass access to shallow water for dawn and dusk feeding forays.

Another spot to look for is a creekbed point. Here, the former creek made a sharp turn, leaving a peninsula of land isolated in the middle. Not only will the undercut bank opposite the point hold bass, but the point itself will draw bass up into it to prowl weedbeds and drowned timber. By fan-casting plastic worms, grubs, and tailspinners or still-fishing with jigging spoons or conventional jig-and-pig rigs, some of the big boys can be fooled with far less trouble than in other parts of the lake. Also, since bass usually use creek channels as a highway through the lake, the number of fish in such places is fairly constant. So even if you occasionally take a few for the skillet, it won't necessarily mean you've fished the spot clean.

It virtually always pays to work the spots where the old creekbed ran through a wooded area. Since impoundment, these areas have been reduced to woody snarls of downed limbs and standing stumps that line the old channel, creating excellent ambush points where many bass can take refuge in a small area. Especially good are the places where the old woods came to an end and the creek entered grassy terrain. There are at least three spots here that are likely to hold schools of bass: the last bend in the channel before it exits the old woods, the first bend after the woods, and the edge of the old timber line.

WHERE TWO OR more of these old streams converge into one main run, bass cruising the channels often get stuck in traffic at the intersection and have to wait there until the bottleneck clears. Since the current where the old creeks joined was strong, the intersection is now deep and rocky. You can either drop jigs into these holes or cast a plastic worm, grub, or other bottom-hugging bait to the far side of the channel and retrieve it slowly down one bank, across the bottom, and up the opposite bank. Even inactive bass can hardly resist a bait walked slowly past their noses.

An unusual channel structure that can also be productive is the creek saddle. Basically, it is a point where two bends of the old stream came close together and were separated by a small finger of land. These creek saddles can hold schools of fish even in the hottest weather if they are in deep water. The school will usually congregate over the point of land between the two bends with many of the bigger bass lingering just below the undercut dropoffs in either side. To properly work the area, cast onto the top of the structure and work the lure down either side into the bends. More active fish will strike near the dropoff, while inactive bass will wait until the lure drops down the channel bank. But don't spend too much time here if you get no results after 30 minutes, because schools tend to come and go in this type of structure.

Finally, one of the best spots in any creek channel is where old roads crossed over the water. These can be located easily by using a good topographic map of the lake and can be identified on a graph or depthfinder almost as easily. Aside from the fact that the old concrete roadbed makes a hard bottom available to those species that prefer it, such as smallmouths, the old drainage ditches and submerged bridges and culverts offer perhaps the best habitat for the lake's trophy fish. The main problem is figuring which type of structure you have found.

As a rule, wider parts of the former creek were spanned by small bridges, while narrow parts were equipped with concrete culvert pipes. The bridges will frequently be decayed or even gone by the time a reservoir is a decade old, but the concrete culverts last until they silt over. Both will usually hold a small but remarkably weighty group of bass.

Working these spots requires a slightly different technique. For starters, fishing them with horizontal-moving lures such as crankbaits and plastic worms will seldom work. Bass holding in such structure are almost always wary, inactive feeders that need a bait dangled in their faces to get their interest. This calls for the use of jigs or jig-and-pig rigs dropped no more than a few feet from the opening of the culvert or bridge. Worked meticulously around both ends of the structure and perhaps tipped with live bait, this jigging method will eventually yield some remarkable bass. But the nearness of all that concrete and steel makes it easy for a big bass to break

your line. So bring the bass up as far as you can immediately after setting the hook. You can always play him out once you have him away from cover.

Fishing a lake's creek channels involves more than drifting along and walking a worm on the bottom. By fishing only certain parts of the channel, you will get better results and bigger fish with far less wasted time than the usual hit-and-miss tactics tried by hot-weather anglers. And I'm sure you can think of something to do with the time you've saved.

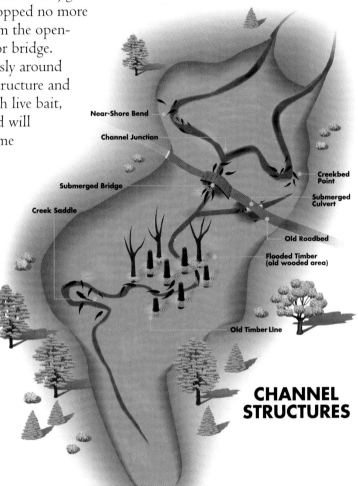

Near-Shore Bend

Channel Junction

Submerged Bridge

Creek Saddle

Creekbed Point

Submerged Culvert

Old Roadbed

Flooded Timber (old wooded area)

Old Timber Line

CHANNEL STRUCTURES

by Bill Volkart

COLD-WEATHER
Bass

BASS DON'T STOP BITING
IN NOSE-NUMBING TEM-
PERATURES; THEY SIMPLY
REQUIRE A LITTLE COAXING
AND A LOT OF PATIENCE.

*U*NLIKE HOT-WEATHER bass fishing, winter's harsh conditions necessitate some changes in our fishing routines if we are to be successful. When cold weather finally settles in, most bass hold in the warmer waters of the hypolimnion layer of the lake, particularly in the first months of the season when its oxygen levels have yet to be depleted. This is particularly true where deep creek channels cut across the bottom, since schools of shad and other forage fish use the same routes in their annual migrations upstream. At these depths, which can easily be 20 to 40 feet and more, only lure designs that dive deep and move slowly enough to be of interest to the sluggish bass will be effective. This includes heavy jigs in the 1/2- to 5/8-ounce range, often tipped with pork trailers, jigging spoons, tail-spinners, and grubs, all of which work best when fished in areas that hold large schools of shad, a primary food of early winter bass.

To get the attention of lethargic, cold-weather largemouths, you need to put your offering right in front of their noses. You have some leeway using this method, since winter-time bass tend to gather in large schools and suspend vertically rather than horizontally, but when I say close, I mean *close.* When fishing steep dropoffs, try to get as near as possible to the edge before you send the jig down. It may seem a negligible distance to move your boat, but that 2 or 3 feet can be crucial. Provided you keep the jig skirt long (short-skirted jigs lack sufficient action at slow retrieve speeds), pay attention to the distance that the bass must travel to take the bait, and fish the creek channel walls slowly and systematically, you should soon be rewarded with some big bass.

Sooner or later, usually after cold rains have flushed the shad from their upstream forage areas, the bass will disperse in search of other food sources. Remaining shad and crayfish will congregate on bluff points near creek channels, along steep, rocky shoreline areas, and, in warm spells, among timbered points in shallower water. During these periods, bass will move to follow the forage fish and can be caught on single- or twin-spin lures using a pork trailer as an added enticement. To be successful, however, these lures must be fished slowly.

A slow presentation also applies to deep-diving crankbaits designed to resemble crayfish. Even bass that have switched over to crayfish as the bulk of their winter diets will not go out of their way to chase one down. If you're fishing a rocky shoreline or a rock bar that is about the right depth for your diver, work the lure slowly and methodically along, bashing the lip of the crankbait into the bottom to make it resemble a crayfish's natural behavior. The tapping sound as it collides with the rocks, plus the slow, jerky presentation, convinces most cold-water largemouths (and smallmouths) that an easy meal awaits.

Just remember to keep your rod tip low while working crankbaits. At a depth of 20 feet or more, the slack in the monofilament will take quite a pull to tighten up and if you don't have the vertical space to snap the rod up, setting the hook firmly will be difficult. When you do turn up a smallmouth instead of a largemouth bass and would like to take advantage of your good fortune, you might want to switch to a doll-fly with a pork trailer. Work the jig over the rocks in short hops, keeping in good contact with the lure, and the bass will do the rest.

You should also pay close attention to your gear when angling for wintertime bass. When the temperature hovers at or below the freezing mark, wet monofilament can cause an icy slush to permeate your spool and water leaking into the reel itself can seize up gears and release mechanisms easily. Be sure to take backup equipment to replace them if you can. Even the line itself can develop an icy coat and will have less elasticity than when used under warmer conditions. Unless you recently filled the spool, watch for wear and nicks to the line. If you think weakened mono loses big bass in the summer, just think what that battered line you put on last spring will do when it's 30 degrees and a 4-pounder takes your lure.

Speaking of lost fish, catch-and-release fishermen must also take note of the colder air temperatures this time of year. Unless you plan to eat what you catch, don't keep the fish out of the water longer than necessary and avoid any attempts at amateur photography. By the time you shoot a few pictures, your bass will be history.

Besides the fish, your own comfort and safety should be carefully considered when angling for winter bass. Because you will be spending long hours in the open with nothing to shield you from the wind, warm clothing, preferably layered, and a good windbreaker are mandatory. Gloves with the fingertips cut off will keep you comfortable yet allow you to tie jigs and untangle line without a lot of fuss. Since your feet and your head are responsible for most of the body's heat loss in cold weather, heavy socks, water-resistant leather shoes, and a warm hat or stocking cap are essential. If it's bitterly cold, take the time every now and then to get out onto the shore and walk around a bit and perhaps build a small fire if one is permitted where you are fishing. Both will help your circulation and give you a welcome respite from the weather so that you can return to the lake ready for a few more hours of angling. Naturally, a thermos of hot soup or stew and another of coffee or hot chocolate will add some much-appreciated body heat of their own.

Also, try to avoid going out on the lake by yourself and always wear a good quality life jacket, regardless of your swimming ability. Taking a tumble into a cold lake can quickly rob the body of heat. Even with help around, make sure to take along a sealable plastic bag or large jar containing dry matches and tinder to build a quick fire if the need arises. Unless you are close to your car, the trip back down the lake soaking wet can give you a bad case of frostbite or hypothermia at the worst and a dose of the shakes and a possible bout of pneumonia at best.

But even with these threats to your comfort and safety, angling for bass in the winter is a rewarding experience. A day on the lake free of crowds and waterskiers is a real treat in these times of heavy fishing pressure and recreational use of our waterways and the bass are less wary after getting a vacation from the same aggravations. By keeping warm, fishing your lures slow and deep, and getting them as close to the suspended schools of bass as possible, you will have just as much luck, if not more, than you ever had on a hot August afternoon.

By Cliff Hauptman

Getting the Jump on BASS

EARLY SPRING IS THE TOUGHEST TIME FOR ANGLERS
WHO HAVE TO OUTGUESS BOTH THE WEATHER AND
THE FISH. BUT THERE ARE TRICKS YOU CAN USE TO
COME OUT AHEAD.

THE LAKE HAS BEEN frozen all winter, the bass torpid, and the plants dead. Now, however, the spring air has warmed to the point where all you can think of is fishing. Fortunately, the water temperature has also crept up to the point where you have a realistic chance of getting a winter-starved bass to chase your lure. Even so, your favorite lake has become a strange and unfamiliar place. All the weedbeds are gone. You cruise over to where those vast patches of lily pads were last summer only to find nothing but shallow water obviously devoid of bass.

Last summer, when the season was mature and the lake had its full growth of aquatic greenery, finding bass could be a simple matter even for the beginner armed with just an elementary knowledge of bass behavior. The lake itself practically took you by the hand, led you to its weedy gardens, and said, "Fish here."

Clues were everywhere and readily apparent. But what about now? Where in the world do you fish?

The answers come from knowing what bass are doing at this time of year, when water temperatures and hormonal changes control their movements as tightly as a choke-chain and leash control a frisky pup. Warming waters stimulate hormonal activity that brings bass ever closer to spawning until, by the time temperatures in the prime nesting sites reach the low 60s, the bass are ready to put all their attention and energy into reproduction. Until then, while water temperatures are still in the 50s, bass spend a great deal of time moving in and out of the shallows in search of food and comfortable temperatures.

Every angler is familiar with the fickleness of spring weather. You're bundled in a wool shirt and down vest as you launch your boat in the morning, but by the time you take a midday break for a sandwich and soda, the heightening sun and lack of shade have you peeling off layers of clothing. By midafternoon, you may be down to a T-shirt, but 10 minutes later, as another errant cold front drops out of Canada on gusting winds, you may find yourself

wrapped in down and wool once again, blowing on your hands, and heading for the dock.

The bass are subject to those same weather changes, which result in the continually changing water temperatures that can keep bass in nearly constant motion at this time of year. The savvy angler also stays in constant motion, checking and rechecking the likely spots—the extreme shallows in dark-bottomed, northwest coves, and the edges of the nearby dropoffs.

In early spring, the sun is still mainly in the southern part of the sky throughout the day, just as it was all winter. From that angle, the northern end of a lake receives more direct sunlight throughout the day than does the southern end. More sunlight causes higher water temperatures, earlier plant growth, and, in turn, more dissolved oxygen. All of those

factors attract food species and, therefore, the bass themselves, which are also seeking those same conditions for their own comfort.

Dark bottoms absorb and hold warmth better than light-colored bottoms, and so will hold the warmest water. In addition, dark bottoms usually indicate the presence of a layer of silt, often overlying a sandy bottom, and those are the preferred nesting conditions of large-mouth bass.

Coves in the northwest corners of lakes are also well protected from cold-front winds, which typically come from that direction in the spring, and so these sheltered coves with their additional warmth are where you should be to find the bass.

Later in the season and throughout the summer these coves will be thickly carpeted with weeds and lily pads, providing perfect cover for post-spawn bass whose only interest by that time will be filling their bellies. Now, though, there is no such cover, so the bass will be relating to the only edge available—the shoreline. This is the time to work as tightly against the banks as possible, tossing your lures into every little pocket that might possibly hold a basking fish. The bass are plentiful, hungry, and ready to feed, but you have to be precise and deliberate with your casts.

I have found that the best types of lures for this kind of fishing are weedless spoons or weedless jigs with a pork-end trailer, or a Texas-rigged plastic worm. All of these lures have in common their weedlessness and vertical action. You will need a dependable, weedless lure not because of aquatic weeds—there are none yet—but because of the bankside vegetation; if you are not regularly tossing your lure into an overhanging bush, you are not working close enough to the bank. You also want a lure that will fall straight down against the bank and can be hopped along the bottom on the retrieve. The spoon, jig, and worm are ideal.

Last spring, as I paddled my johnboat into the inner reaches of a shallow cove that is impenetrable later in the summer due to the dense growth of lily pads, I kept my eye on my temperature gauge, noticing the slow but steady rise—by fractions of a degree—as I advanced into the cove. Finally, I reached the innermost portion and found, to my surprise, that a substantial channel entered the cove. I moved into its mouth, the temperature still rising, and began to see large and pulse-quickening V-wakes caused by fleeing bass. As cautiously as a heron, so as not to spook any more fish, I tossed a weedless jig down the middle of the channel and hopped it judiciously back, expecting it to be attacked from all sides. Nothing. Had I alarmed all the bass within range? I tried again, right down the center, hopping it back. Still, there were no takers.

I tried a longer cast, farther up the channel where it began to bend out of sight to the right. The lure flew a couple of feet farther than I had planned, and instead of landing near the middle of the channel again, the lure hit the bank at the far side of the curve and then dropped in. Serendipity! The take was subtle but immediate.

I landed a big male and tossed the jig only a dozen feet away, but against the bank again. Bingo! I had discovered the secret. In that relatively warm channel, which measured only about 50 feet long and 12 feet wide, I caught and released nine hefty bass before the commotion turned off all the others that were crowded in there.

Naturally, I was back there the next day, but overnight, the temperature had taken one of its typical dives, and the day was downright cold. Monitoring the surface temperature of that same cove showed a drop of 4 degrees from the previous day. The channel's temperature had fallen, too, and the bass were not there. I moved back out to the mouth of the cove and worked the dropoff with a single-bladed white spinnerbait that I allowed to flutter down the drop. The plunge in temperature had not diminished the bass' appetites, I soon learned, but it had caused them to move nearly 100 yards to a different environment.

Throughout the day, I visited similar dropoffs at the mouths of coves and continued to catch bass. But at about 3 P.M., when the temperature of both the air and the water had begun to make noticeable headway toward a warming trend, my success on the dropoffs shut off like a spigot. I motored back across the lake to my secret channel and, sure enough, the bass were there, proving that movement is the general order of things for bass at this time of year. The successful angler will be the one whose strategy entails the continual rechecking of spots throughout the day. More than at any other time of the year, an area that proves unproductive in the morning may be the hotspot of your dreams after lunch.

Early spring is arguably the easiest time to catch bass. They're actively seeking food after a lean winter; they're beginning to get aggressive in preparation for spawning; and they're likely to be less cautious of anglers, having been relatively unmolested for a few months. And now that you know how to find them, get a move on!

By Ken Schultz

How Bass Anglers Can Beat
THE HEAT

THE BASS OF SUMMER ARE THE SAME FISH AS ALWAYS.
YOU JUST NEED TO PICK YOUR TIMES, PLACES, AND
LURES WITH EXTRA CARE.

NO MATTER HOW happy you were to see summer arrive, by now you no longer appreciate the heat. The lake feels like bath water, and those small summer joys—croaking bullfrogs, screeching kingfishers, and the splash of feeding fish—have become dampened by thunderstorms, tornadoes, snakes, sunburn. . . and fishless summer days.

Just hearing water lap against your boat is no longer reward enough. You want to catch some bass. But nothing seems to work: the water's too hot; the lake's too busy; the fish have been pressured too often; there's too much bait for them to eat; they've gone too deep; they've gone into cover… In short, they're doing the things that bass do to beat the heat.

But there are ways that bass fishermen can beat the heat, too.

First, fish where the water might be colder. This method is opposite to the way you fish in early spring, when cold lakes and reservoirs are heating up. Then, the warmest water and best action are often found in shallows in or near tributaries. But by midsummer, the surface water is hot everywhere, so bass look for the comfort of places with shade or depths that are cool—and to catch fish, so should you.

In reservoirs with little vegetative cover but enough depth for a thermocline, most of the bass will be deep. Find their comfort zone, and put your lures down there. In shallow lakes with little depth, the fish head for the lily pads, weeds, moss, hydrilla, and other cover that offers shade and food. Some small waters also contain springs with considerable temperature difference. If you've ever been swimming and felt the change in temperature as you passed through a spot, you've probably encountered a spring. Bass like these places, too, and if you locate cool spots, that's where you should fish.

If you're planning a fishing vacation, keep in mind that, in general, the water is much warmer during summer in the South than it is in the North. Shorter growing seasons in the North make for somewhat smaller bass than you'll find in Southern states, but cooler nights make for generally cooler waters, and bass are within reach throughout the summer.

Actually, bass are seldom out of reach no matter how far down they may go, but fishing effectively for them when they're very deep is not easy. Most of us just aren't very good at it or don't like that type of fishing. But since we, unlike bass, can move from lake to lake, when fish go too deep in the water you usually fish, head for another that's smaller. Most bass anglers are primarily casters who enjoy tossing lures to specific places where fish might be hiding, and like the art of retrieving and manipu-

lating their lures. They are most adept with this, have more confidence when fishing this way, and are more successful.

Even in the heat of midsummer, the average angler will do better on small lakes and ponds because bass there have fewer places to hide and are relatively shallow and accessible. The "trick" here is to use your best skills and forget that you're fishing under difficult conditions.

But not everyone has the opportunity to fish small bodies of water. Those who don't might try to schedule their outings for times when their local lake isn't crowded. A major impediment to successful midsummer fishing is competition for space. Speedboats, sailboats, personal watercraft—even swimmers—can create noise, waves, and roiled-up water. Try to fish typically busy areas when the commotion is at its least. This means early in the day, at dusk, at night, at midweek, and when the weather is cool or cloudy or rainy.

If you have to fish in the middle of a bright, hot Saturday or Sunday, then you might try places that are least trafficked by other watersports fans. Backwaters, stumpy rivers, flooded timber, rocky reefs and shoals, and similar places where it's difficult to do anything but fish are good choices. There is no guarantee that the bass will be biting, but most anglers stand a better chance in such quiet places than anywhere that boat after boat churns by.

Fishing early and late in the day and at night is about as old a rule for summer bass fishing as you can find, but it holds true for most people in many bodies of water. This is not to say that you cannot have good bass fishing during the day. But slightly cooler water, less traffic, and more personal comfort make early and late angling a good bet for maximum enjoyment and productivity.

Besides time and place, many other factors can influence midsummer bass fishing. When the going gets tough, try using light tackle. Not in heavy cover or murky water, of course, but when you're fishing deep in clear water and using small lures, light is right.

By midsummer, bass have been subjected to a lot of fishing pressure, so a fine-diameter line can be important. Use 4- to 8-pound-test line with jigs, small plastic worms, spoons, spinners, small crankbaits, and minnow-imitating surface plugs. You can use spinning tackle for some of these lures, and bait-casting tackle for others, but be careful to pick the right lures. A few decades ago, a shallow-running plug or surface lure was synonymous with midsummer bass fishing. Now it's a jig or plastic worm.

Have the bass changed? In a sense they have. They're not as easy to catch as they were when fewer people were angling. But they're still the same fish. You can still catch them shallow or on the surface, just not all the time. The key is to pick your times and places carefully and to fish the right lures in the right places at the right times.

This sounds simplistic, but it's too often ignored. You shouldn't expect to catch bass on a surface lure in the shallows in the middle of a hot sunny day unless a school of baitfish has been herded there. But in low light, surface and shallow plug fishing will not only catch bass that are temporarily shallow, but also get them to come up for your lure. When bass are deep, however—generally, over 10 to 12 feet—you have to get down to them, though the tactics you use will be dictated by the terrain, the cover, and the situation.

Jigs and plastic worms are prime midsummer lures because they're fished on the bottom and worked slowly and deliberately through the cover.

But even the most popular lures don't always do the job. Sometimes it pays to be unconventional. Last summer on a Northern pond, I discovered that small spinners worked just as well as larger, more conventional bass lures. My wife and I were fishing for panfish, letting the spinners sink to just above the tops of heavy grass and moss, and though we did well with panfish, we caught just as many bass, perhaps because they'd seen the other lures more frequently. A 1/16-ounce spinner, normally used for trout and panfish, looked tiny in the mouth of some of the bass, especially our largest, a 5-pounder. On a spinning rod and 6-pound line, that fish provided great sport, and a perfect way to beat the heat.

Day or Night Lake

When is a bass lake better for night or day fishing in midsummer? The busier the lake in the daytime, the more likely it is to provide better fishing at night. Conversely, a lake with little or no daytime boating or swimming, such as many private lakes with no-outboard restrictions, would either be poor at night or at least as good during the day.—K.S.

By Mark Hicks

Pointing the Way to
BASS

HAVING TROUBLE FINDING FISH? DON'T WORRY. A CLOSE LOOK AT THE SHORELINE OR A GLANCE AT A CONTOUR LAKE MAP SHOULD TURN UP A GOOD STARTING POINT.

LARGEMOUTH BASS ARE harder to find than catch, especially on big waters where they have so many options. Some bass prefer the shallows. Others rarely leave deep water. They may follow schools of baitfish in open water or hang out near wood, weeds, rocks, manmade cover, or a variety of bottom structures. They could be anywhere, but they certainly are not everywhere.

Whenever you find yourself overwhelmed by the variables, remember this: Points point the way to bass.

Points funnel bass to predictable locations, and if you learn how to recognize points and fish them effectively you'll suffer fewer fishing slumps.

Once you get into the habit of looking for points, they'll jump out at you everywhere. The most obvious point is a ridge of land that juts into a lake. The ridge usually continues under-

water, offering structure that attracts bass. The shape and composition of the point indicate what lies beneath the surface.

Less obvious are underwater points that offer no clues above the surface to tip off their whereabouts. One way to find them is by studying a contour lake map.

Anywhere the contour lines draw a finger that points to deep water is a potential bass magnet.

HIDDEN HOTSPOTS

NOT ALL POINTS are visible to the eye or drawn on lake maps. These must be found by scouting with a depthfinder, a time-consuming chore that requires a degree of luck. The effort, however, may turn up points that yield exceptional fishing for untapped bass.

In late fall, winter, and early spring, concentrate on main lake points that drop sharply into deep water. The vertical drop allows sluggish cold-water bass to move deep or shallow by traveling a short distance. Work a jig dressed with a pork frog along the drop-off and be prepared to do battle with some of the biggest bass that live in a given lake.

When bass begin moving shallow in the spring, switch to "secondary points" in coves and creek arms, especially points that feature hard bottoms, such as sand, marl, or pea gravel. Secondary points are smaller than main lake points and they do not drop off so deeply. Bass stop and feed at secondary points as they make their way back to spawning grounds and some eventually spawn on these points. Spinnerbaits, crankbaits, topwater minnows, and plastic lizards are high priority lures for secondary points.

In the summer and early fall, many bass vacate the shallows and set up shop on long, sloping, main lake points that gradually reach out to deep water. These extensive points provide large feeding areas and ample forage which bass require during summer.

TACKLE POINTERS

THE ONE-TWO PUNCH for long points is a big, deep-diving crankbait and a Carolina rig. (A Carolina rig consists of a 1-ounce

A ridge of land that juts into a lake usually continues underwater, offering structure that attracts bass. Less obvious underwater points can be found by using a contour lake map.

sinker followed by a two-way swivel, an 18- to 36-inch leader, and something on the order of a 6-inch plastic worm or lizard fixed on a worm hook.) Deep-running crankbaits and Carolina rigs can be cast long distances and they get to the bottom fast, helping you cover large points more easily. The bass may be scattered, but they often concentrate on key areas, such as the edge of a drop-off, a stump row, or brushpile.

Also give points special consideration when casting to shorelines. The mouth of a small cove offers mini points on either side of the opening. Riprap breakwalls fronting marinas end in points that regularly produce bass. Even a subtle point along a featureless bank can be a consistent bass producer.

Points are just as productive when fishing weedlines. Since weeds grow along depth contours, wherever you find a point of weeds, it reveals a point on the bottom. The dual points formed by the bottom and the weeds make such places especially appealing to bass.

The point is, if you look for points and fish them regularly, they'll lead you to more bass. Get the point?

By Jim Dean

Trading Linemen for
LUNKERS

FOR ANYONE WHO'D RATHER CATCH BASS THAN A GAME ON TV, OVERTURNING A FEW TIRED FALL FISHING TRADITIONS IS THE FIRST STEP TO SUCCESS.

Cold weather will make bass relocate—but not to the shallows. Concentrate on middle depths for the best fishing.

BY MIDAFTERNOON, the temperature had climbed into the 70s, and I had already taken off my flannel shirt. We were experiencing one of those glorious Indian summer weather patterns marked by cool nights, warm days, brilliant blue skies, and the drowsy buzz of insects along

country roads. As Jack Avent and I positioned the boat to fish a line of docks, we could hear a Saturday afternoon game on TV coming from one of the old cabins.

"Don't you just love football?" remarked Jack. "There isn't another boat in sight."

There was good reason to savor having the water all to ourselves on such a handsome day. Later that afternoon, one of the bass I released weighed 7½ pounds. Indeed, we had been enjoying periods of superb fishing ever since Labor Day. Similar success in recent years has convinced me that many anglers have fall bass fishing figured all wrong.

Tradition says that autumn's cool weather wakes up those fat largemouths that have been lethargically mopping their brows in deep water. Rejuvenated by moderating water temperatures, bass supposedly sense the coming winter and move to the shallows where they gorge like teenagers at a church picnic. All a bass fisherman has to do—or so we're told—is toss out the goodies and success is assured. Yet, haven't you often been skunked on crisp, gorgeous days when conditions seem perfect? Small wonder many fishermen hit the couch in front of the tube. The truth is that, contrary to its reputation, fall bass fishing can be frustrating and uncertain.

It doesn't have to be that way. If you're willing to violate a few tired traditions by changing your tactics, autumn fishing will live up to its reputation.

LOVE HAS NOTHING TO DO WITH IT

THE FIRST TIP is to stop thinking of fall as the flip side of spring. We forget that largemouth bass in autumn aren't driven by a compelling urge to spawn in the shallows. Without the persistent tug of lust, bass are in no hurry to leave their comfortable, deep summer homes as long as they have plenty to eat—certainly not as early as Labor Day. That traditional beginning of fall fishing is just a calendar date. Often, it's still blazing hot over much of the nation, and you can't expect consistent success by simply reverting to shallow-water spring tactics on the heels of the first cold snap.

Sure, you can catch plenty of small bass that way, but those fat females in the lunker category don't have a good reason to move out quickly. Throughout much of the season, you'd do far better to spend more time fishing deep.

In early fall, it may help to forget that it's fall. Instead, continue to use summer tactics, fishing deep structures in open water until those spots stop producing fish. When this happens depends on where you fish; in the mid-Atlantic where I live, good fishing in deep water can last well into October, and occasionally later. During this period, summer rules still apply, and down to about 12 feet, deep-diving crankbaits like the Poe's, Mann's, Bagley's, and Bomber Model A are especially deadly. If the fish are on deeper structure—15 to 18 feet or more—it's easier to reach them with a Texas- or Carolina-rigged worm or other soft-plastic lure and a 1/2- to 1-ounce weight.

MOVING RIGHT ALONG

AS THE WATER begins to cool significantly, and bass leave their deepest summer haunts and become harder to find and catch, it pays to continue fishing middle depths, especially for large bass. Except when they're spawning, lunkers seem to have a natural distrust of shallow water and in the fall big fish can find plenty to eat along food-rich, secure contours at 6 to 10 feet. Cold weather will make bass relocate—but not to the shallows. Concentrate on middle depths for the best fishing. Since the fish have little reason to move into the shallows on any permanent basis, don't expect to find them there with any consistency.

Particularly during midday, I like to concentrate on middle-depth structure such as points, creek channels, and deep banks. The best spots will have cover on the bottom, so Jack and I look for brush, stumps, submerged trees, or riprap. Since we're fishing down to 6 to 10 feet, we slightly modify our summer tactics. Soft-plastic worms and salamanders often still produce, and so do deep-diving crankbaits, but as the leaves begin to drop and the water grows colder, we expect increasing success with spinnerbaits and rattling lures like the Rat-L-Trap. For crankbaits or rattle baits, I find that chartreuse, silver, or pearl produce best, but brilliant reds and oranges can also do surprisingly well. For spinnerbaits, combinations of chartreuse and white are hard to beat.

Docks and boat houses are also good bets in the fall, especially if they jut over deep water. One fall a few years ago, while fishing an old millpond, I retrieved a 1/4-ounce Rat-L-Trap deep alongside the pilings at the end of a boat house and had a vicious strike. Moments later, a huge largemouth bass rolled on the surface.

"That's a double-digit fish!" Jack shouted. The line sliced the dark water and the fish rolled a second time closer to the boat. We clearly saw its massive head and belly. Suddenly, the lure squirted back to the surface, and we sat looking at it in disbelief. I hated to lose that bass, but at least I had the satisfaction of knowing that I had been using a tactic that could produce such lunkers. It's doubtful I would have hooked a fish that size had I been fishing along a shallow shoreline.

FOLLOW THOSE FISH

THERE IS ONE surefire way to find big bass that will take you into both deep and shallow water. On big impoundments and reservoirs, there are often huge populations of forage fish, such as threadfin and gizzard shad. Find the shad and you'll find the bass, too.

The movement of shad begins in late summer or early fall with schools of the baitfish suspended over deep water near points or other irregular bottom structure. There, they can easily be located with a depthfinder. Some schools will show up as large, dense masses of fish, but what you're looking for are the schools that appear as irregular, patchy groups. This may indicate that the shad are being scattered by feeding bass. Deep-diving crankbaits and rattle lures that can reach these suspended fish often work. For schools that may be 20 feet deep or more, a jigged forged spoon such as the Shorty Hopkins is your best bet.

As the water cools, the shad will begin a subtle but increasingly obvious movement into shallower water. Phil Cable, another fishing buddy of mine and a big-lake specialist, loves to key on this pattern. When the shad begin to move shoreward, he follows them. He knows from experience that by mid-fall, perhaps a bit later, the shad are likely to spend several weeks at depths of 5 to 10 feet near the shorelines of coves and creeks off the main lake. He particularly likes to fish those depths along the outside edges of hydrilla or other weedlines with spinnerbaits or crankbaits that imitate shad, working them slowly and frequently stopping the retrieve. And he's learned that fishing is often best on windy, overcast days.

By late fall when the weather is often quite wintry, the shad may be in only 2 to 3 feet of water, and Phil looks for bass around stumps or other woody cover in the heads of shallow creeks or coves. Spinnerbaits and shallow-diving crankbaits that can be worked slowly are your best bet.

Jack and I also regularly encounter the same schooling activity on smaller lakes and millponds—even on farm ponds—where golden shiners are present. A school will normally contain bass all about the same size, usually up to about 2 pounds, that can be lots of fun to catch on light tackle. Generally bass will gang

up to feed near points or over structure, but you'll sometimes find them in open water chasing bait on the surface.

When schools are on top, a Zara Spook, Pop-R, or Baby Torpedo—my favorite is a transparent Torpedo—fished rapidly to imitate frightened bait will usually do the trick. For schools feeding beneath the surface, lures like the Little George or Rat-L-Trap are hard to beat. Another killer for schooling bass is a Bagley balsa Small Fry Shad, particularly in a naturalistic silvery color. Jack and I have also found this lure highly effective for larger bass when they're in relatively shallow water (5 feet deep or less), especially late in the season.

Fall can be a tough season, sure enough. but that's no reason to stay inside. If you simply must keep up with that pigskin business, carry a radio in the boat. And if I happen to be your companion, bring earphones.

Weather; It Matters

I like to take fishing trips toward the tail end of warm Indian summer weather that hangs on late in the season; the best time to be on the water is the day before the arrival of a strong cold front that promises to drop the temperature from the 60s or 70s into the 40s. If warm, moist air brings cloud cover ahead of the front, you may get fast action all day. Jack favors those last few hours before a front passes.

"I want to start out wearing a T-shirt, and end up in an insulated jumpsuit and rain jacket with the wind whistling," he says.

At such times, bass may hit anything you throw, but a Rat-L-Trap or spinnerbait worked along a windy shore or riprap can be especially deadly. There's nothing leisurely about this kind of fall fishing, but it's one of the times you can expect to find big fish in relatively shallow water.—J.D.

By Mark Hicks

UP A CREEK

Unaffected by the fall turnover, these small waterways offer some of the most consistent bass fishing of the season.

For some, the phrase "up a creek" means being in hot water with your boss, spouse, or possibly a teacher—definitely situations to be avoided. Successful bass anglers, however, have no qualms about being up a creek in the fall, because this is where they find the most consistent largemouth fishing of the season. When the annual BASS Masters Classic was held in October, as it was for many years, almost every tournament was won up a creek, regardless of where the event took place.

Many types of creeks offer excellent bass fishing in autumn, particularly the feeders of large impoundments, the tributaries of large rivers like the Ohio and Mississippi, and tidal creeks that empty into major river systems which eventually mix with the oceans, such as the Potomac River that flows through Washington, D.C. and the St. Johns which swings north through Jacksonville, Florida.

Productive creeks for bass abound across the country. Be mindful, however, that not all creeks have exceptional bass potential. Key in on larger creeks (although small ones may be excellent at times) because large creeks have more fresh, incoming water, are more fertile, and attract and support more baitfish, which, in turn support more bass. This is generally true of creeks in any water system.

Wherever you're planning to fish, obtain a good lake or river map, mark the largest creeks, and concentrate on them when the weather cools in the fall. The most obvious feeder in an impoundment, the major incoming stream or river, is a good bet. Also worth investigating are other large creeks, especially those in the upper ends of an impoundment farthest from the dam. Keep in mind that water up a creek usually doesn't stratify during the summer, so it is not adversely affected by the fall turnover, as are deeper main lake areas.

Many bass in major creeks are resident fish that never leave, but their numbers are frequently bolstered come fall by scads of bass that swarm out of the main lake or river, following the schools of shad migrating upstream.

An abundance of baitfish in a creek is more than helpful—it often is crucial to a productive outing. You may run into a bass or two in creeks, or areas of creeks, that have few baitfish, but if you want to tangle with lots of bass, make locating baitfish one of your highest priorities. Be persistent. Continue searching for baitfish, working up the creek until you reach its upper quarter section.

Bear in mind that during the morning these forage fish may be deeper and visible only on your depthfinder. In the afternoon, when the sun warms the water, they tend to rise and group up in schools that are easily visible. I've seen creeks where the water's surface was solid baitfish from bank to bank. In these instances, it is common to see bass busting their prey on top.

If baitfish are not present, check out other creeks until you find them. Another point to remember is that the bass will follow baitfish. The section of a creek that was packed with baitfish and bass one day may be devoid of activity the next. Don't panic. Simply motor up or down the creek until you relocate the baitfish and, chances are, you will also relocate the bass.

One of the nice things about creek fishing is its uncomplicated nature. Normally it involves casting to shallow, visible cover with standard bass lures and tackle. Fallen trees are primary targets, especially those that reach from the bank into deeper water. If you're fishing an impoundment that has been drawn down, you'll generally find the bass relating to the very ends of the tree tops. Other excellent wood cover includes stumps, brush, and snags on shallow flats.

John Schwarzel, who runs Schwarzel's Marine on the banks of the Hocking River near its junction with the Ohio, would never overlook a snag up a creek. Schwarzel, a highly regarded bass angler in these parts, has been fishing creeks for most of his fifty-two years and dotes on them in the fall.

"When I'm fishing a snag," he says, "I like to bring a spinnerbait or a crankbait right down alongside the cover, since you stand a better chance of exposing your lure to the bass. I also try to match my lure to the size and color of the shad that are present. And don't worry if it's shallow. As long as there's enough water to cover a bass's back, that's plenty."

Another of Schwarzel's primary locations is any creek bend where logs, branches, leaves, and other debris have piled up, creating excellent cover for bass. A hook-guard jig tipped with a pork or plastic craw, or a Texas-rigged worm, serve well for penetrating the labyrinth and tempting the bass below.

Pay special attention to small inlets trickling into creeks and tributaries, since they tend to attract bass. When bass are actively feeding in the mouth of an inlet, they are highly susceptible to spinnerbaits and crankbaits. When they are less active, you may find them directly up or downstream, holding tight to the nearest available cover.

That cover may be wood, but it also could be man-made or natural broken rock, possibly weeds, or even bridge pilings. The water beneath bridges that passes over creeks has often been dredged out and is deeper. In many cases, particularly when fishing very shallow creeks, these and any other deep holes you come across can concentrate bass. The downstream sides of points and shoals also are prime locations.

One of the keys to your success with creek bass in the fall is to thoroughly fish all the different types of cover available until you determine which ones are holding bass. Concentrating on these preferred covers will vastly improve your odds. Because bass tend to roam and change locations frequently in some creeks, you may have to go through this process of elimination regularly to keep abreast of what the bass are doing.

Basic tackle should include a flippin' rod with 20- to 25-pound line for getting into the thicker cover, a medium-heavy bait-casting rod for casting spinnerbaits, plastic worms, and jigs, and a medium-action bait-casting outfit for crankbaits. Since most creeks have stained water, go with heavier line, say 15- to 20-pound-test.

Spinnerbaits of all sizes are superb creek lures in the fall. I prefer a 1/4-ounce single spin with a No. 4 Colorado blade when fishing snags on shallow flats. For deeper water and steeper banks, I usually switch over to a 1/2-ounce spinnerbait with large tandem willow-leaf blades. A variety of crankbaits that run from 2 to about 8 feet deep will handle most creek fishing situations, although there may be times when deeper divers could come into play.

With both spinnerbaits and crankbaits, you can't go wrong with patterns that include the color chartreuse.

Hook-guard jigs and plastic worms are the other mainstays for creek fishing. When fishing waters that are noted for producing big bass, don't hesitate to go with a sizable jig, something on the order of a 1/2- to 5/8-ouncer with a plastic 4-inch craw for a trailer. For some reason, however, smaller 4- to 6-inch plastic worms seem to be more productive for fall creek fishing. Stick with darker hues for both jigs and worms, such as black, brown, blue, and purple.

Moving water is often a variable to consider when fishing creeks, especially in tidal rivers and in reservoirs where water is pulled to generate power. Savvy anglers take advantage of this; they know that the flow encourages bass to feed aggressively and forces them to hold tighter to cover and in eddies, making their locations easier to predict. Larger objects that form substantial current breaks, such as large fallen logs, wide stumps, prominent boulders, pilings, and shoals are the most likely structures in this situation.

Bass will position themselves behind objects that break the flow and create a pocket of slack water where they may hold without fighting the current, yet be in an ideal position to dash out and engulf any tidbits that wash past them.

Many anglers fail to tempt moving-water bass because they cast directly to visible objects, and their offerings are pushed downstream before the bass have a chance to see them. It's crucial that you cast several feet upstream of the object so your lure has an opportunity to sink or dive to the bass's level where it can trigger a strike. Remember that a bass always will be facing into the current and that a lure swimming with the flow appears more natural to the fish. The faster the current, the tighter the bass will be holding to the cover and the more critical your presentation will be.

The best fall creeks are located far from public launching ramps. They receive less fishing pressure because fewer anglers are willing to make the long runs necessary to reach them. Once you head up a remote creek, don't become discouraged if shad are not readily apparent and strikes from bass are not soon forthcoming.

Keep going until you reach the very headwaters, if necessary. There you may find shad almost thick enough to walk on, along with hordes of agreeable bass. This is one instance when being up a creek will be a stimulating experience instead of a stressful dilemma.

The most-asked question in all of bassdom just may be "What are they hitting?" And given the profusion of lures now on the market, "what" could be just about anything: a double willow-blade spinnerbait with a silicone skirt, a chrome spoon, a jig-n-pig, a deep-diving "softshell craw" crankbait, a concave popper, a twin-prop topwater plug, or a soft-plastic curl-tail grub, to name only a few.

Let's say you select the ubiquitous plastic worm. Now, do you use it Texas-rigged, Carolina-rigged, or Do-Nothing rigged?

Do you flip, or pitch?

And if your choice is a topwater plug, on the retrieve do you make it jerk—or pause, stop-and-go, or walk?

So many choices. How do you choose wisely?

Well, experience is a great teacher, and this section draws on writers who have more than a century of combined fishing expertise under their well-worn belts. Furthermore, they are experts at explaining what they do, and how you can do it too. Following their lead will help you focus on proven techniques, which can turn you from a question-asker to an answer-giver.

SINCE 1895

FIELD & STREAM

THE SOUL OF THE AMERICAN OUTDOORS

By Mark Hicks

BASS LURES...
All Dressed Up

THINK OF TRAILERS AS
BASIC NECESSITIES, NOT
FRINGE BENEFITS.

DRESSING UP THE
hooks of your bass lures is
no act of whimsy. The right trailer can
transform your lure from ineffective to irresistible—and your day from so-so to super.

"Trailers almost always catch more bass," says Bill Alley, Sr., a veteran bass guide from Sebring, Florida, whose clients seem to have a knack for catching 10-pound-plus largemouths. Alley's favorite spinnerbait trailer is a soft-plastic, 3-inch twin-curlytail grub in pearl. First, he pinches off the head of the trailer, then he slips the body of it over the shank of the hook, leaving the bend and the point of the hook to protrude from between the grub's twin tails.

The twin-tail grub gives Alley's spinnerbait more bulk and action, providing a bigger, livelier target for fish to hit. It also adds buoyancy which slows the lure's fall and lets it run closer to the surface with slower retrieves.

Trailers let you add contrasting colors or match colors to given water conditions. Some hold rattles to add the attraction of sound. Pork rinds and scented soft-plastic trailers tantalize a bass's senses of smell and taste, and their lifelike feel encourages bass to hold on longer, giving you more time to set the hook.

Yet for all the things a trailer can do, it won't do much unless you make sure it's in balance with the primary lure. Oversized trailers make spinnerbaits and buzzbaits roll up on their sides, and they kill the action of jigs and weedless spoons. A trailer should complement the lure, not overpower it.

The twin tail that Alley dotes on works well with spinnerbaits weighing 1/3 ounce or more, but for 1/4- to 3/8-ounce spinnerbaits, a 3-inch single-tailed grub is a better match, and a 2-inch size is best for 1/8-ounce spinnerbaits. You can also simply break off the head of a curly-tailed worm and use the tail as a trailer.

Big largemouth bass hammer 5- to 7-inch eel-type worms when they undulate behind a heavy spinnerbait with a big, willowleaf blade. You should fish this rig slow and deep over submerged weeds. This same lure combination lights up big smallmouths when it's retrieved briskly just beneath the surface.

A 4-inch plastic split-tail eel is a good all-around trailer for most spinnerbaits. It dances nicely and lets lures run true at any speed. Cut it down to match smaller spinnerbaits.

Buzzbaits often benefit from wide trailers that give them more lift, such as a pork frog or a plastic version of a pork frog. For a more realistic dressing, strip the skirt off a buzzbait and dress the hook with a plastic shad that features a wobbling tail. The latter setup is less apt to run true, but it can be worth the trouble.

Carry an assortment of pork frogs in various sizes. Small frogs give jigs a subdued profile that appeals to finicky bass. Large frogs make for big, slow-sinking jigs—just the thing for heavy bass in dense, shallow cover.

The fat on a pork-rind bait makes your lure more buoyant. Trim part or all of the fat off for a faster sinking lure; leave it on to retain a slower fall. Trimming the fat can also improve the trailer's action, as does deepening the split between the tails. To prevent a pork trailer from sliding up the hook and blocking the point, break off a piece of plastic worm and thread it onto the shank before attaching the pork.

Plastic jig trailers offer an alternative to pork, especially in warm weather. Particularly good are plastic crayfish, which mimic the real thing right down to the pincers. Weedless spoons have little appeal to bass without trailers. Pork frogs and eels, or plastic swimming-tail worms and grubs are just a few excellent additions to these lures. Just be sure to balance the spoon and the trailer for best results.

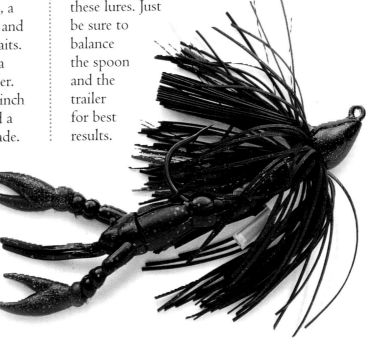

By Mark Hicks

FLIPPING

BASS HOLDING IN TOUGH COVER REQUIRE ACCURATE CASTS AND PRECISE PRESENTATION. FLIPPING IS A TECHNIQUE DESIGNED TO PUT YOU IN COMMAND OF SUCH SITUATIONS.

FLIPPING IS A specialized technique that provides a means for extracting bass from imposing cover such as dense brush and overhanging limbs. In fact, it is the most efficient system ever developed for precise presentation of lures at close ranges out to about 20 feet. The long, stout 7½-foot rod and heavy line lets you zip jigs, plastic worms, and similar lures from one small opening to another with an underhand swing. When done properly, the flipping motion is smooth and effortless.

1) CAST YOUR LURE out about the same distance you will be flippin'. You must start with the lure well out in front of you to get the pendulum motion started.

2) TURN THE REEL'S SIDE plate toward the water before starting. Pull the lure out of the water and draw it back toward the boat by lifting your rod tip while pulling on the line with your free hand. Be sure the reel spool is engaged.

3) LOWER YOUR ROD TIP as the lure begins to swing past you. Continue to hold the line with your other hand so the lure can reach the back of its arc without touching the water. At the peak of the backward swing, the rod's handle must extend above the wrist on either the inside or outside of the arm. The line between the rod tip and the lure should remain straight throughout the cast.

4) IN ONE FLUID MOTION, sweep the rod tip up slightly above horizontal and, at the same time, tug the line slightly with your free hand to propel the lure toward the target. Feed line fast enough to keep the lure close to the water, but don't allow any slack line.

5) BRING YOUR FREE HAND BACK toward the rod, allowing the weight of the lure to pull the line through the guides.

6) JUST BEFORE THE JIG reaches its target, dip the rod tip slightly and snub the lure's progress by stalling the line with your free hand. This makes the jig assume the proper posture and land lightly. Your free hand must maintain control of the line throughout the cast.

By Glenn Edwards

Bombarding BASS

"INCOMING" HEAVY JIGS CAN STARTLE BASS INTO AGGRESSIVE STRIKES.

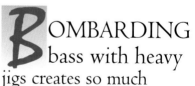OMBARDING bass with heavy jigs creates so much commotion that bass may simply flee the area—or they may decide to fight back, aggressively attacking these lures when lighter jigs and other lures are ignored.

I often bombard bass in 3 to 8 feet of water with a ½-ounce hook-guard jig tipped with a standard No. 11 pork frog. Most fishermen would consider this too heavy for such shallow water. On several occasions, however, I've caught largemouths in the 3- to 5-pound class with this lure while anglers casting lighter jigs ahead of me were going fishless.

Although many anglers reserve jigs for cool-water seasons, heavy jigs also fare well in the summer. The key is their fast sink rate, which allows for a speedy retrieve that often appeals to warm-water bass that have grown more active. During the summer, many bass move out to main lake structures near deeper water, and the speed of a heavy jig also reduces the time it takes to locate them.

Jigs weighing ½ ounce or more cast like bullets. This is advantageous for covering large structures, such as sloping points that reach far into the lake before dropping off. Make a long cast, let the jig touch down, and then work it back with a bottom-hopping retrieve that makes the jig jump up sharply.

The heavy jig pummels the bottom and serves as an effective structure finder as well as a bass catcher. It also helps you determine whether the bottom is hard or soft, and when the jig thwacks a stump or rock, this information also is relayed through the rod tip.

When you feel the jig contact an object likely to harbor bass, bump the cover several

Heavy jigs are perfect for flipping to holes in submerged weeds.

times with the jig before jumping it over the obstacle. This trick works especially well with stumps. Keep in mind that your line is draped over the top of the stump, or one of its roots, and that the jig is bashing the backside of the cover. Hold your rod tip at about 11 o'clock and shake it back and forth while maintaining a semi-tight line. This will make the heavy jig knock forcefully against the wood, which will attract any bass nearby.

On many occasions, a bass will snatch the jig off the back of a stump. If you don't get a response after knocking on wood six or more times, pop the jig over the cover and let it sink. If a bass has been watching the jig banging against the stump, this sudden darting motion generally provokes a reflex strike. Be alert as the jig falls, since it may never reach bottom.

When fishing submergent vegetation, shorter casts are necessary to prevent constant fouling and help you detect strikes. If the weeds are sparse or clumpy with lots of openings, you may be able to make longer casts and work the jig against the vegetation similar to the method used when fishing stumps. Shake the jig several times after it has made contact with the weeds, and then snap it free with a sharp jerk that rips it through the vegetation, cleans the jig, and sparks bass into action.

When drifting over submerged weeds that are visible from the surface, make short pitches to holes and openings. These often appear as dark spots. The heavy jig will plummet to the bottom of these holes, allowing you to tempt bass with a few hops before you move on to the next opening.

When fishing over matted weeds, or submerged vegetation that has few openings, you may have to go up to a ¾- or 1-ounce jig in order to break through the weeds and into openings below where bass may be lurking. In this situation, avoid casting altogether and simply plop the heavy jig into the greenery near the boat. After the lure has broken through the weeds, be sure to work it up and down several times before retrieving it and plunking it down a few feet farther along.

A plain black or brown jig with a black-and-blue No. 11 pork frog has come through for me on many lakes and impoundments across the country. There are countless other effective color combinations, however, especially when you get into plastic trailers, such as craws and twin-tails which have proven to be deadly. I prefer a 6½-foot medium-heavy bait-casting rod with a long handle and 14- to 17-pound line for most heavy jig applications.

Heavy jigs even score well in ultra-clear waters, such as the canyon impoundments out West, even though this is where tiny finesse lures and light lines predominate for bass. Greg Hines, a noted professional bass angler from Gilbert, Arizona, has had excellent results with unpainted football-head-shaped jigs weighing ⅝ to 1 ounce. The football head is molded sideways onto the hook and the line eye protrudes through the middle of the lead. This makes the jig drop sharply with little forward gliding.

"Because the football head falls more directly," says Hines, "it keeps your line tighter, giving you more feel at greater depths."

HINES NORMALLY DRESSES his heavy jigs with plastic spider skirts and 2½- to 3-inch plastic twin tails. Some of his most productive colors are green, smoke-sparkle, and a purple skirt combined with a chartreuse trailer. When fishing one of these jigs on 15- to 17-pound line and a 6½-foot medium to medium-heavy bait-casting outfit, Hines regularly catches bass in 35 to 40 feet of water and has taken them as deep as 55 feet.

Hines cautions against using a rod that is too stiff when fishing deep, because it may load and unload so quickly while you set the hook that you'll lose the constant pressure needed to work the hook into the bass. When Hines senses a strike in especially deep water, he quickly cranks in line until he feels the weight of the fish and then sets the hook with the rod.

"A 1-ounce jig is a fairly fast bait even when you're fishing in 50 to 60 feet of water," points out Hines. "A lot of times, I'll use it almost like a crankbait—keeping on the move and covering a lot of water, while the heavy jig makes a lot of vibration and water movement in the depths. That's the whole key to the bait, really."

The heavy jigs produce well for Hines in the summer when bass are holding on extensive main-lake points in 35 to 40 feet of water. He makes long casts, lets the jig bash into the bottom, and then hops it along with a fast retrieve.

"Sometimes I'll use the 1-ounce jig in water that's only 10 to 15 feet deep. I throw it out as far as I can, which is a long way with a 1-ounce jig. After it hits the bottom, I reel it like crazy, then stop and let it sink to the bottom. Then I reel it again and stop. It's like fishing a crankbait. You'll be reeling and all of a sudden there's a fish on it."

Of course, there will be days when bass will have nothing to do with heavy jigs, just as they routinely shun all other lures at times. But when speed, noise, and commotion put the fish in a fighting mood, bombarding bass with a heavy jig is one of the fastest ways to catch them.

By John Merwin

HELP *from the* BASS LAB

For this kind of research, all you need is plenty of H_2O and a rod to stir things up.

to do with largemouth bass fishing, but only if you ask the right questions in the right spots.

Quiet water usually provides the best answers, so a small pond is a must. This might be a rural Texas stock tank, a suburban golf-course pond, or any of the generic bass ponds ubiquitous nationwide: too small for water-skiers, too muddy for swimmers, and perfect for undisturbed bass fishing.

*B*ASS LABS ARE PLACES where chunky guys in green-and-black "coats" hang around evaluating whatever happens to drop in. They'll give you a detailed report on almost anything having

My own bass lab is a small kettle pond with lots of stunted largemouths rarely longer than a foot. Your local pond may have bigger fish, but getting answers from a number of fish is more important than hooking a big one. You'll learn more without big-fish pressure, which is why we're at the bass lab in the first place.

Here's one type of experiment brought to the experts: Floating/diving minnow-type plugs often work best when allowed to rest near bass cover and then carefully twitched. This means keeping precise track of the plug, which is difficult because the motionless, dark-backed plug is hard to see. Many trout fishermen favor white-winged dry flies like Royal Wulffs simply because such flies are easy to spot. The same principle might work for a surface plug, I reasoned, so I used some model-airplane enamel to paint a broad white stripe along the top of a small floating-minnow plug. I didn't know if the bass would mind, so I left an identical plug unpainted and took everything down to the pond for testing.

I first made a few casts with the standard dark-backed plug, wanting to know if the bass would respond with the occasional swirls and strikes I had come to expect when using this lure. If for some reason the "control" version didn't work, I'd have to try at a different time. The bass were coming as predicted, however, so it was time to switch plugs.

Even when floating a long cast away, the white-backed plug stood out like small-town neon on a dark night. The advantage was immediately obvious, and a few twitches made it more so as the plug disappeared in a generous swirl. The bass was hooked on the forward treble, having hit straight from the side. There was no hesitation, no tentative nipping at the tail hook. Over the next hour, the painted plug performed at least as well as the control version, and I learned a great deal. Now both small and large painted versions of the same plugs are part of my basic gear, along with a few unpainted plugs—just in case.

Light spinning gear loaded with 8-pound mono allows me to match assorted small lures with the pond's small fish, but I don't use just any lures. Because many bass baits—both hard and soft—are made in a wide range of sizes, I can often transfer the results of my small-pond experiments to larger waters with otherwise identical bigger baits and heavier line. If you're going to experiment, it helps to use lures that offer this versatility.

As much as anything, the bass lab signifies a way of thinking, a willingness to experiment on quiet water where your results will be most evident. Just remember that if one of your methodical experiments with lures, tackle, or tactics happens to work, that doesn't guarantee success with the same method all the time or everywhere. But you have learned that the method will work at some times and places, which is better than relying on just plain dumb luck.

My lab assistants helped me radically change the tactics I use with soft-plastic baits. I often fish weedy bass water using a Texas-rigged plastic worm, as is common, but with no bullet sinker or other added weight. This means the essentially weedless worm fishes between the surface and a foot or two deep—depending on how it's retrieved—allowing me to twitch it slowly in weedy pockets and then slither it over the lily pads—all of which is more difficult with a weighted rig. It's a simple, effective method for shallow-water largemouths in typically heavy cover.

A 6- or 7-inch worm is relatively light, so this method requires spinning tackle for the easiest casting. Unfortunately, most strikes come in weedy jungles, and even 12-pound mono—which is about the heaviest practical line weight for casting in this case—is often not strong enough to hold larger bass away from tangles, and breakoffs are common. I thought the new high-strength small-diameter polyethylene (Spectra) lines might provide a solution, so I set up a simple test.

I first tried a small purple worm on light monofilament versus the same worm fished on Spectra. Some of the bass grabbed and quickly spit out the worm fished on mono—as usual—but wouldn't touch the same bait on the opaque, light green Spectra, which looked like clothesline in the clear water. Somewhere in the spring flood of tackle catalogs, I'd seen waterproof markers offered for camouflaging braided lines. This seemed reasonable, so on my next trip to the pond, I took two Spectra-spooled spinning rigs, having first used a permanent marker an one to make the last few feet of line black instead of green. The difference was remarkable: black Spectra got almost as much interest as my former monofilament setup, while the green version literally went untapped.

The kinds of things you can test in this fashion are almost limitless: one lure color against another, size variations, and different plastic bait designs are a few more examples. Just keep your variables at a minimum, and experiment during a short timespan so that changing weather conditions don't rewrite the equation.

A simple approach gives the clearest answers. I'd been wondering, for example, if the new "flavor enhanced" plastic baits would work any better than my old purple standards, and so I took that question to the bass lab, too. I rigged unweighted worms—flavored and unflavored, but otherwise identical—on a pair of light spinning rods, and tried the old-style version first. The fish took this worm as they had on past days, sometimes interrupting my careful twitches with a fast bump-and-spit routine that often left me yanking empty water.

Next came the otherwise identical flavored worm fished in a similar fashion. Not only did the bass grab the flavored worm and not let go, but a few actually swallowed it. This was almost too good, and the problem quickly became setting the hook fast enough to prevent gut-hooking the fish.

That lab report carried a bonus later made evident when I occasionally took novices bass fishing. Most recently this was a friend up from the city for the weekend, a woman who knew about fishing but had done relatively little. Learning to rig her own worm came quickly, as did basic spin-casting. "Just toss it over toward shore," I told her, "and reel it slowly back while you twitch the rod tip once in a while. When you feel a pull on the line, you've got a fish."

After a cast or two, her rod was bent, and a little largemouth came splashing against the side of the canoe. She managed to untangle the worm, hook, and fish, which she released with a mile-wide grin. "Wow," she said, "if everybody finds out bass fishing is this simple, all those different equipment manufacturers will go out of business!"

It's not always that simple, of course, but sometimes it can be—with a little help from the bass lab.

Walking baits, which include a variety of hard-bodied and soft-plastic models, can be made to dart, wobble, twitch, jerk, and otherwise move fast, slow, on the surface, or just under it, according to the mood of the fish you're after.

By Ken Schultz

IT'S ALL IN THE JERK

THESE LURES WILL ALMOST ALWAYS FAIL IF YOU JUST REEL THEM IN. BUT JERK THEM AROUND ARTFULLY, AND BASS WILL EAT THEM UP.

*I*N SUPPORT OF THE notion that some things go full circle, consider the Heddon Zara Spook. This surface lure was very popular with warm-water anglers back when gear was less sophisticated and anglers had to rely on their retrieval skills to get the most out of many lures. Then tackle improvements made the process easier, and lures like the Zara Spook that fishermen really had to work faded away. But in the late 1970s the Zara (and imitators) reemerged as a good topwater tool for those who liked to do more than just chunk and wind.

Nowadays the Zara is just one of the various lures, touted for their ability to catch bass in heavily fished spots, that have to be manipulated, not simply reeled in. This isn't always made clear; in fact, the No. 1 reason why bass fishermen fail when using these lures is the lifeless way they retrieve them. To catch bass, you first have to catch their attention. And that's where the jerk—plus the twitch, pause, stop-and-go, and walk—comes in.

Although jerking is often associated with surface plugs, the retrieve is also useful with floating/diving plugs, deep divers, and some soft plastics. Walking baits like the Zara must be fished in a jerking style, but different surface lures such as floating minnow plugs (most of which can be used on *and* beneath the surface), can be fished in a twitching manner, and alternating this with jerking is highly effective. Some minnow floaters, such as a Bill Lewis Slap-Stick, rest tail down and don't swim on a straight retrieve, but must be jerked and twitched in short strokes to make them dart forward a few inches at a time.

One of my favorite bass lures is a 5-inch minnow-style Bagley Bang-O-Lure Spinner, which has a single spinner on its tail; it's best to jerk this quickly when the bass are aggressive, and twitch it lightly when the fish are timid. This lure has a rear spinner that creates a little more commotion than the average minnow plug, yet it swims well because of its lip, so when the fish won't hit on a subtle jerking or twitching motion, they often will hit when the lure is jerked sharply just under the surface.

Some plugs that are used almost exclusively beneath the surface are designed to be fished with a steady retrieve, which imparts an enticing wobbling action. This includes all types of crankbaits and diving plugs. Such a retrieve is fine for fish that are aggressive or unfamiliar with fishermen and their lures. For wary fish in heavily fished waters, you often have to make otherwise good-swimming lures act like they are wounded, disoriented, and vulnerable. One of the best ways to do this is with a below-surface stop-and-go retrieve. Another effective tactic is to jerk the lures, which makes them dart suddenly. A slow darting or jerking action, in which baits move forward in short, unalarming bursts, is often preferred, but you can also induce strikes by effecting very quick "frantic" motions caused by making the plug bolt forward, stop momentarily, then bolt forward again.

Diving plugs are usually fairly buoyant, and they rise when stopped momentarily. This can draw strikes and is an effective way to work these lures in and around submerged vegetation, stumps, and standing timber. However, I prefer to fish a floating/diving lure that either suspends or rises very slowly. If you've watched small fish underwater, you'll see that they swim a short distance and stop, then repeat this, usually staying at the same level or perhaps drifting downward.

Some hard-plastic or wooden lures, because of their balanced design or because of their density, can mimic that sort of behavior when they're stopped during the retrieve, whether as a result of jerking or simple stop-and-go reeling. A few plugs are made to suspend. You can doctor many plugs to decrease or neutralize their buoyancy. A previously popular method of doing this with wooden lures was to put shot into the body. A new and increasingly popular way is to use Suspen-Dots.

These are small strips or circles of lead tape made by Storm Lures. Applying the tape judiciously provides a plastic or wooden lure with the means to rise very slowly or to suspend in place. Either way you have a lure that, when jerked and stopped, behaves a lot like a forage fish.

A prime attribute of soft-plastic jerkbaits, which have become popular in recent years, is their ability to suspend or sink slowly under the surface and to be deliberately erratic when retrieved. Most soft plastics, particularly worms, are known for their slithering, shimmering, undulating action, worked primarily on or close to the bottom, so these soft-plastic blobs didn't impress many anglers when they first came along.

When I initially tried Lunker City's Slug-O (the original in this genre) and later many other soft-plastic jerkbaits, I wasn't impressed. But these lures do catch fish, and I began to wonder why bass (and pike) would go for lackluster plastics.

I began to see that the soft-plastic lures look a lot like wounded, darting fish when they are jerked, and also when paused, because they descend slowly like a dying fish. One advantage to soft-plastic jerkbaits over hard versions is that they are rigged with a single hook embedded inside, which makes them reasonably snag-resistant and easy to fish in heavy cover, especially vegetation. Lily pads, with their frequent openings on the surface and ample clearance below, are very good spots for these lures. Another advantage is that soft-plastic baits will go deep so you can make them get down to the fish rather than try to make the fish come up to the lure.

Some soft-plastic jerkbaits dart well from side to side, while others have a more canted darting-rolling action. You should experiment a bit with hook size and placement to achieve the desired effect, and also be attentive to proper rerigging after a fish has been caught.

Generally you have to keep your rod tip down and pointed at the water when retrieving these lures. You can jerk lures quite well on a raised rod (angled at an 11 to 12 o'clock position) but only when the lure is a long distance away; as the lure gets nearer, it will not sweep or dart well from one side to another unless you point the rod down. A low rod angle also helps set the hook.

Keeping the rod low, jerk or sweep the tip toward you while taking up slack line with the reel handle. This is a coordinated move. Using bait-casting tackle held in your left hand and with the rod tip pointed toward the water, use your left wrist to jerk the rod from left to right in short bursts. Just after each jerk, your right hand makes a turn on the reel handle, taking up slack. It is very important that you reel after you've yanked the lure, because the way jerk-baits are balanced, the nose usually drifts to one side, and will dart in that direction when jerked. Then when the lure is paused, the nose drifts the other way and the lure can be jerked in that direction. But when you reel before you jerk, the lure straightens out and heads toward you instead of toward the side. By jerking first and then reeling, you're taking up slack line, which doesn't affect the lure. This may seem like a small difference, but it is crucial to get-ting the lure to be most effective.

Coordination and rhythmic timing are the key ingredients to perfecting the jerking retrieve. When you've mastered it, you can walk a lure above or below water at a high speed, although fast retrieves are less productive below the surface than above it. Slower retrieves are generally most effective with all jerkbaits, and in some situations, such as fishing around a particularly good bit of cover, a slowly walked surface lure, fished in tantalizing jerks, pro-duces savage strikes.

Sensing when to modify your retrieve is a key element of successful fishing; sometimes it's a result of observation. Seeing a fish swirl after a lure, for example, may indicate that it isn't aggressive, but is attempting to stun prey rather than devour it immediately. Usually, slowing a lure down, making it more tantaliz-ing, or creating a tease is necessary to provoke a solid strike.

Jerking is especially effective on large-mouth bass, but it also works well in appropri-ate situations for smallmouths, stripers, pickerel,

northern pike, muskellunge, peacock bass, snook, and redfish.

So get over any ideas you have that soft-plastic blobs and stickbaits or jerkbaits aren't glamorous, and put some effort into your retrieves. You'll be glad you turned to a jerk the next time a hard-to-get bass grabs your lure.

About Tackle

Although bait-casting tackle is most commonly used with jerkbaits, spinning gear is also appropriate with small lures and when fishing in open water for bass, especially smallmouths. The reel itself presents no problem, except that with some the erratic action will cause line to pile up on the spool irregularly and there may be an occasional snarl. Periodically make a long cast and retrieve the lure straight back under direct tension to prevent this, or get a better spinning reel that has more positive line pickup.

Long rods are in vogue with bass anglers, but long rods (7- or 7½-footers) aren't as good for jerking because the rod must be pointed low toward the water much of the time and they are too long for that. Also these retrieves are sometimes done in thick cover (a timber stand, for example) that isn't conducive to long-rod use. A 6-footer is about right, and while it should have enough backbone to handle hard hooksets, it should also have a fast-action tip.

A rod with a quick taper that provides some limberness in the tip is better than a stiff-tipped one for getting the proper action out of a lure. An elastic or stretchy line also produces good lure action, but since it makes hooking more difficult, there's a tradeoff. It's helpful to use a rounded snap with some jerkbaits, or a loop knot, to increase swimming action and side-to-side movement. Many jerk-baits (especially the surface version) work better with less direct line-tie tension.—K. S.

By Nick Lyons

LARGEMOUTH MAGIC

WHEN A BIG BASS BUSTS UP TO THE SURFACE TO ENGULF A TOPWATER BUG—PRESTO!—YOU'VE GOT LIVING DYNAMITE IN HAND.

GREEN-GRAY, CHUNKY, with a gourmand's palate and beastly eating habits, the largemouth bass has probably given more pleasure to more people than any species other than its little cousin, the bluegill. I am addicted to the brute.

Largemouth bass are not finicky or fussy or easily scared. They will eat anything they can get their big jaws around. They mean business when they strike, but grow bored—as I do—with the ensuing fight. Yet there is just no freshwater sight as heartstopping as a truly big largemouth busting up for a hairbug on a muggy night, blasting the surface with the sheer weight and ferocity of its strike, sending a lathered fan of silver in every direction, and hustling away like a spooked muskrat when it realizes it's hooked.

I caught my first largemouth bass as a teenager at a summer camp in the foothills of the Berkshire Mountains in New York. In the beginning, it was by mistake—while slowly hoisting out a 3-inch bluegill. Later, it was on purpose—with night crawlers and crayfish, minnows caught in a bread-baited jug, then spinners, spinner-and-worm combinations, Jitterbugs, and Pikie Minnows, and finally on big deer-hair or molded-body bugs. The bugs were merely a plump turtle-shaped body with crisscrossed clumps of hair for the four legs. That's still the bug I use most, nearly half a century later.

When I found the fly rod, I never let it go. Even in those early days when I half-tossed, half-slammed a bug out on a level line—sticky from too much grease—I was hooked by the rise of a largemouth to a surface bug. You saw everything. The expectation—as the fly lit, twitched, wiggled, waited, stuttered, and rushed headlong toward you—was thrilling. I could barely cast the big thing 30 feet, but when I got it out its presence on the calm surface of the lake mesmerized me. Several times fish struck (and came off) while I looked away, dreamily, and I learned then, for all time, to rivet my eye to that little object on the surface and keep it there for dear life. And once I learned never to

look away, I was hooked to the bug; I felt its every movement, and waited, every moment, for that explosion on the surface.

I also liked the way the fishing was done. I didn't have to fish all day, find fish in deep water, or use hardware of such weight (and number of hooks) that the fight was diminished. I liked an old rowboat that went at exactly the speed I propelled it; I liked the oars making their rhythmic sound against water and oarlock; I liked the constant sight of the shoreline with its myriad of shapes and forms: eelgrass, lilypads, old rotted stumps, fallen trees or branches, jutting rocks, dropoffs, points, rocky flats, coves, islands, channels, overhanging brush or branches, and so much more. I did not fish to a fish, as I would for trout; I fished to a spot where a fish might be. Slowly I

★ MOSTWHIT HAIR BUG: Some thirty-five years ago, when I first discovered how realistic and effective deer-hair bugs were, I began developing this fly. I wanted a soft surface fly that landed with a natural *plop* on the water and would "sit" with hook and legs down. I also wanted a pattern that would catch bass while motionless or as it crawled, kicked, or fluttered across the water surface structure. In addition, I wanted the bug to "pop" when needed.

Tall order, but this fly does it all. I like it in yellow, fruit cocktail, black, frog, and red head in sizes 10, 6, or 1/0. A slow, irregular retrieve works best; let it sit awhile, then twitch, pop, and pause as you pull the bug along the shoreline. You won't have to wait long for results.

★ WHITLOCK WAKING MINNOW: This is a deadly effective surface swimming fly that precisely imitates surface-feeding or crippled

minnows which bass find irresistible. It's especially deadly where shad, shiners, and sunfish are abundant.

It's a perfect choice when you see minnows scattering across the surface as bass bust into them. Slowly and erratically moving it around shoreline structure as if it were trying to slip away from a monster bass also produces consistent results.

★ PENCIL POPPER: This water-squirting, hard-head surface fly with a slender body profile is my favorite when bass want to chase surface minnows. It works great when schools

of shad, shiners, smelt, or top minnows are abundant.

Although it catches fish when it's just sitting or twitching on the surface, it's especially hot when it's darted, skipped, popped,

and changed directions with rapid line strips and rod motions. I use it in 2-inch and 4-inch versions in silver-and-white or brown-and-gold finishes. These colors imitate most minnows that bass eat daily.

★ DAVE'S DIVING-SWIMMING FROG: Nothing beats surface bugs for sheer pleasure and excitement, unless it's a floater that also dives below the surface on command. Such a fly adds almost a fourth dimension to bass bugging because of its special repertoire. When retrieved, it dives and swims, and when paused, it rises back to the surface. In doing

so it perfectly imitates so many of a bass's favorite prey— frogs, crippled minnows, water turtles, water snakes, small ducklings, etc. This frog, like the Mostwhit Hair Bug, is realistically frog-soft and when cleverly manipulated, swims, crawls, hops, pops, and dives through the watery surface structures where big bass hang out, spring, summer, and fall.

★ WHITLOCK HARE JIGFLY: I wouldn't feel right, after recommending the above top-water patterns, if I didn't slip in one underwater bottom-jigging design. Even on the best surface fishing days, there are lots of times

when big bass insist on dining right down on the bottom in 3 to 20 feet of water.

When fished on a floating bass's bug line and a 10-foot knotless leader, the Hare Jigfly, with its fantastic feel and water-action, is a deadly big bass producer. I like to cast it next to the shoreline or beside a flooded tree and let it sink to the bottom, then ever so slowly hop or jig it a few inches at a time into deeper water. Carefully watch and feel for a subtle tap as the bass sucks the jig in off the bottom, then set the hook quickly and hard–it may well be the biggest bass you'll ever hook on a fly.—*Dave Whitlock* learned the spots, all of them, by getting strikes in certain places, none in others. You did not pitch a fly and let the current take it to a trout, but cast to a stump or a patch of weed and then, by wiggle and pop, tried to induce a fish to come and play. It was great fun. It was leisurely—and dramatic.

Largemouths don't go in for the acrobatic displays so common to smallmouth bass—angling away from the boat as they come up from the depths and then leaping once, twice—high and wriggling. No, largemouths are heavyweights—one-punch knockout artists—and even the smallest play hard, with bad intentions.

The magic of largemouth fishing comes at dawn or dusk when a pond is mysterious, moody, and silent. In the very early morning, after a night on the prowl, big bass can be anywhere. And they're looking for food. I've seen one blast the gently floating plug a friend had left in the water while he untangled a backlash, an hour before dawn; I've seen their streaks and bulges among the weeds; I've had them storm a bug dozens of times, at any of a dozen different moments during a retrieve.

I like to get down to the dock by 4 A.M., before there's any light other than the moon's on the water. A loon calls; faintly, a dog barks. The water, what I can see of it, is flat calm and, in summer, light mist circles above it. I whisper to my friend. Neither of us wants to make the slightest unnecessary sound, even when we leave the car, a couple of hundred feet from the dock. We slip gear into the wooden rowboat, ease oars into their locks, untie the joining rope, and push off. I barely allow the oars to touch the water, just dip their tips gently against the surface. It does not require much more to propel the boat. Only a couple of dozen feet outside of the dock area, I bring the oars in, and we both scan the dark waters for the best place to cast first. My friend is using a plug, I the long rod. He casts far out into the deep water, toward the center of the pond; from the bow, I pull line off my inexpensive fly reel, false cast twice, and cast toward the faint outline of the shore. I can see the shoreline brush, a few rocks, but not much more. On my third cast the water breaks and bursts, as if someone has thrown in a cherry bomb, and I feel the satisfying weight of a good bass. It does

Big Lures, Lighter Rods

For the bass bugger who is armed with a typical 8- or 9-weight rod there are several ways to "fish big" with the lighter rod:

• Overload the rod. Slapping a 9- or 10-weight line on an 8-weight rod puts more line belly weight in the air to load the rod at the closer distances normally encountered when bugging. Incidentally, most of today's graphite rods have considerable latitude in accepting line sizes.

• Modify the leader system by cutting back and beefing up. The typical 9-foot factory bugging leader tapered to 8- or 10-pounds is too long and light to turn over a magnum bug. Go for a stubby 6- or 7-foot leader with a 15- or 20-pound tippet. The short, heavy connection usually is not a handicap amid the reduced visibility of brush and weeds where most

heavyweight bass lurk.

• Streamline the bug. "Big" does not have to mean "bulky." A trim and elongated shape is easier to drive and turn over than a boxy profile. An effective image can be created by trimming hackles and rubber legs that lay back in the air when wet, yet flare and pulse on the retrieve. If commotion is needed, remember an aggressive strip will make even a modest concave face chug and pop.

• Learn to single haul. Increasing the line speed with a firm down-and-back pull with the line hand on the forward stroke of the delivery acts as a supercharger to turn over a reluctant bug (especially against the wind). The distance gained by a double haul may not be critical, but the burst of speed and power of a simple single haul can be a real advantage when "fishing big."— *Joe Doggett*

By Mark Hicks

PLASTIC FANTASTIC

THESE SOFT STICKBAITS MAY NOT LOOK LIKE MUCH TO YOU, BUT BASS CANNOT RESIST THEIR ERRATIC LIFE-LIKE ACTION.

THERE'S A NEW LURE on the market that is so bland-looking you'd probably ignore it or dismiss it as worthless if you saw it in a tackle shop—if you haven't done so already. But the new soft-plastic stickbait, with its simple elongated-minnow design, is one of the most unique and effective bass lures to come along in years. Although it appears as though it would be as lifeless as a stick, it performs with an irresistible action that sets it apart from any other lure in an angler's tackle box.

To rig the soft-plastic stickbait, use an offset worm hook and no weight. After tying your line to the hook, thread the point about ½ inch into the lure's blunt nose, and push it out the bottom. Pull the hook through until the hook eye is hidden just inside the tip of the lure, and twist the point around so it faces the plastic. Run the hook from the belly right on through and out the back. When done properly, the lure will hang straight and the hook's point will lie exposed but protected in a shallow groove along the back of the lure, making it virtually snag free. At least two of the half-dozen-plus soft-plastic stickbaits currently on the market feature shallow grooves that hide the hook inside the bait.

Because it takes a strong hookset to embed the large hook, match the lure with 12-pound-test line and a medium or medium-heavy action rod. Some anglers go as high as 20-pound line when fishing around abrasive cover. A 5½-foot baitcasting rod with a pistol grip does an excellent job of serving up the plastic stickbait and imparting its seductive action.

The most common method of fishing the lure is to retrieve it just beneath the surface next to or over any typical weed, wood, or rock cover bass frequent in the shallows. After casting, hold the rod tip to the side and close to the water and work it with a rhythmic twitch-

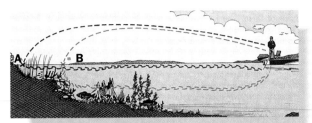

Cast **A** illustrates the basic retrieve for soft-plastic stick-baits, which involves twitching them with a low rod tip just beneath the surface over and near typical bass cover in the shallows. When bass are unwilling to come up to the surface, let the lure sink and retrieve it 3 to 4 feet beneath the surface, as shown in cast **B**.

pause cadence while taking up slack with the reel between twitches. This makes the light-weight lure sashay back and forth with the dog-walking action of a topwater stickbait.

The advantage of fishing with one of these soft-plastic lures is that the lively and erratic action they produce more closely emulates a dying minnow than do hard-bodied stickbaits or any other lures. Since the lure is snag resistant, you can purposely bump it into objects and fish it tight to cover that is off limits to treble-hooked lures. It can be retrieved non-stop all the way back to the boat, or twitched three or four times between longer pauses. During a long pause, the plastic stickbait will dart off to one side and slowly descend like a minnow suffering its death throes. Be alert, since this is when strikes often occur.

You'll see many bass come up after this lure with a fervor that makes for electrifying moments which require crucial execution on your part. If you set the hook the instant the bass swirls, you may pull the lure away before the fish has fully engulfed it. Try to maintain your poise and hesitate for just a second while dropping the rod tip; then take up slack line with a few cranks on the reel, and snap the hook home fast and hard, just as if you were fishing with a plastic worm. Should a bass strike and miss, immediately stop retrieving and let the lure fall. The odds are in your favor that the bass will circle back and take it in.

Bass professionals have been the first to catch on to the benefits of using soft-plastic stickbaits, and these lures have quickly become a dominating force on major tournament circuits across the country. At first, plastic stick-

baits were thought to be mainly for shallow springtime bass fishing in clear water; but they have proven to be much more versatile, readily taking bass from early spring through fall, in murky-to-clear water conditions.

Generally, you'll want to slow the retrieve rhythm in cold water and speed things up in warmer water. At other times plastic stickbaits are more effective when allowed to sink and worked 3 or 4 feet beneath the surface. You won't see strikes with this method, but you will sense a sudden heaviness, which is the tipoff that a bass has taken the lure.

Some anglers clip off the points of nails and insert them into the heads of these lures for additional weight when using subsurface retrieves. Another popular trick is to insert rattles into the tails of the lures to add the allure of sound. For deep structure fishing, rig the plastic stickbait Carolina-style with an 18-inch to 4-foot leader behind a swivel, plastic bead, and a 1-ounce bullet sinker. Twitching the rod tip while dragging the heavy weight over the bottom will impart the lure's erratic action.

Soft-plastic stickbaits are available in sizes as small as $4\frac{1}{2}$ inches, which offer a good alternative when bass are feeding mainly on small baitfish or are too finicky to go for the larger sizes. While basic shad colors are the most popular, these lures are available in a wide variety of color combinations including flakes and two-tones. A variety of soft-plastic stickbaits currently on the market have split tails, flat tails, and realistic baitfish shapes.

For information from the manufacturers of the lures pictured on the preceding page, contact Mann's Bait Company of Eufala, Alabama; Lunker City "Fishing Specialties" of Meriden, Connecticut; Venom Manufacturing of Lithopolis, Ohio; and Culprit Lures of Clermont, Florida.

It would be to your advantage to try a number of these lures on your favorite bass waters. They may not look like much in their respective packages, but when you put them in the water and twitch, they spring to life with an unparalleled action that will readily convince you and the bass that these soft-plastic stickbaits are something special.

By Joe Doggett

PLUGGING ALONG

SURE, SPINNERS, SPOONS, AND SOFT-PLASTIC LURES ARE ALL CAPABLE OF CATCHING FISH, BUT NONE DOES SO WITH THE STYLE AND EXCITEMENT OF THE INTRICATELY SCULPTED & PAINTED CASTING PLUG.

THOSE THAT WERE turned by hand have become collectibles. Even those stamped by assembly have presence and distinction.

They are casting plugs, crafted from wood or hard plastic. They are inspiring to look at and pleasing to hold. They give dignity to casting tackle. They define the sport. Maybe that's why, generations ago, the salty gents with straw hats, direct-drive reels, and "educated thumbs" were called pluggers.

Metal spoons and spinners and the multitude of soft-plastic lures can be excellent choices. But for all their fish-catching capabilities, these lures lack the style of the intricately sculpted and painted plugs.

Plugs are the only casting lures that age with grace. A torn and frazzled worm or a rusted and tattered spinner is discarded with a casual shrug. An old and battered plug, however, is revered. Almost nobody throws one away.

Any good plug has a positive heft and feel. Endorsements aside, you just know it will cast well and fish well. A good plug may drive like a spitzer bullet for distance, or it may arch with finesse for touch, but it will always carry its cast with style. On the retrieve, a good plug will excite bold strikes.

Plugs are at their best on the surface. A vicious topwater strike is a true collision, and a big hit on a "floater" is the plugger's king thrill— an assault on sight and sound and touch that no vague *tap-tap-tap* on bottom can approach.

Effective plug fishing has different tempos and techniques. The traditional approach, and the one that courts the swashbuckling strikes, is the precise delivery to a specific target. Producing surgical strikes on logjams and brushpiles and weedbed pockets demands an aggressive eye and a smooth wrist, the twin strokes of a master. A slow retrieve usually is most effective with a floating or floating/diving plug teased near defined cover.

The surface is the plugger's treasured domain, but plugs can also excel at mid-range depths. A specialized lineup of sub-surface plugs has evolved from the sloughs and shorelines to excel in open water. The wobbling/swimming plugs are superior fish-finders amid the random expanses of coves and flats. The so-called "crankbaits" with exaggerated lips are well suited for combing dropoff edges; the lip digs for depth as it bounces the lure over potential snags such as limbs or rocks. A quick retrieve provides increased efficiency for covering the available water—an advantage over slow bottom-bumping or jigging when fish are scattered.

Fast or slow, shallow or deep, most plugs benefit from stuttered pauses. The steady pulse of a constant speed certainly will draw strikes (as when trolling), but abrupt and staggered pauses that break the flow and impart a "crippled" sensation can produce reflexive hits from trailing killers.

The strikes on plugs usually are solid and the hookup percentages are good; however, the dangling sets of trebles do carry potential drawbacks. The standard-issue rigging of two or three sets of trebles might encourage easy hookups, but the smallish hooks lack the muscle of the large single hook used with most soft plastics and many spinnerbaits and spoons. The loose, swinging trebles can snag brush and weeds, allowing a strong fish to twist free. Another consideration is the tendency of trailing points and barbs to wound and disfigure fish. Finally, the same exposed hooks are a real hazard when excited hands grapple with a wet and thrashing fish. Most barbings almost certainly occur with gang-hook plugs, as opposed to the inherently safer single-hook lures.

Trebles on some plugs can be replaced with single hooks, but almost nobody does this. Big singles look out of place on casting plugs. Perhaps the most practical compromise is to mash flat all treble barbs.

So plugs are not without their problems—or limitations. The rank and file are poor choices for bottom-bumping in deeper water, and there are times when the ability to work the bottom might mean the difference between lots of fish and "slim pickin's."

But numbers are not always the standard that the veteran angler lives by. Fishing remains an adventure steeped in tradition, and as long as the black swamp water beckons and lily pads and logjams look good, there will always be a place for plugs.

Material Matters

Wood and plastic have divided plug fishing into two schools. Tradition favors the former, but practicality supports the latter. Each material has advantages and disadvantages.

Surface and floating/diving plugs carved from wood usually float higher than plastic lures of similar size and shape. Wooden sub-surface swimming and crank-type plugs often exhibit a slower, "lazier" wobble than plastic models. These subtleties can make all the difference when fish need to be coaxed into striking.

Conversely, the buoyant properties of lighter woods, such as balsa, can create casting difficulties. The light, "airy" construction encourages these baits to drift in flight, and the increased punch and velocity needed to drive a cast a distance can cause a backlash. A streamlined profile and weight-forward balance can create superior ballistics in a wooden plug, but a hard-plastic plug will almost always out-cast one made of wood.

Wooden plugs also lack durability. Contact with rocks and logs can crack the finish and dent or cut the body. A heavy tug-of-war with a strong fish might pull the hook screws loose or otherwise damage the relatively fragile riggings. And any customers with teeth, such as pike and pickerel, will inflict cosmetic damage and eventually reduce the effectiveness of the lure.

As a final consideration, plugs crafted from wood and painted by hand are more expensive than similar models stamped from plastic. But, boy, they sure look good! –J.D.

By Joe Doggett

SIGHT
and SOUND

SOME BASS LURES ARE FLASHY. OTHERS MAKE NOISE. BOTH TYPES WORK, BUT IT HELPS TO KNOW WHEN TO USE THEM.

THIS BASS WAS A SMART bomb that lanced through a tangle of brush and a canopy of moss to intercept the passing spinnerbait. Coming out of nowhere, the strike was a masterpiece of efficiency. But what sparked the bass's lightning-quick reaction?

Most strikes are triggered initially by the stimulus of either image or vibration. The angler who understands this can, under a given set of circumstances, simplify his effective lure selection.

All first-string gamefish are aggressive predators that feed on smaller aquatic or terres-

trial animals, and virtually all rely primarily on sight for locating their prey. But a few—mostly ambush-oriented feeders—also depend on sound.

The largemouth bass is one of these. Look at a mature bass. The coloration and profile suggest a fish of weeds and brush, a mugger that hides and waits, using the cloak of subsurface cover as an ally in its attack. What the bass cannot see, it often senses at close but obscured range through its lateral line. The irregular and frantic vibrations of a wounded or struggling creature act as a homing signal, enabling the bass to zoom in accurately on an initially unseen target. This trait has fed a lot of healthy bass—and gotten more than a few into big, barbed trouble.

From the earliest days of Kentucky reels, savvy bass fishermen have known that a lure capable of imparting the sounds of a struggle can be a killer. Under different conditions, however, so can a quiet and realistic offering.

Of course, many good lures offer both image and motion, but under a given set of circumstances, one quality is usually more useful than the other. It is the initial stimulus that encourages the strike. The angler who strives to recognize this becomes more tuned in to the ways of bass. Do not reach with blind faith for a bait just because Joe Bob "nuked 'em" with it last week. Why did Joe Bob maul them? Was he finessing with sight or challenging with sound? Do the present conditions support his choice? If not, try something different as you dig into your tackle box.

Or boxes.

I have toyed with the idea of toting twin tackle boxes, one loaded for image and one for commotion. It is a logical separation, though few anglers approach a lake from that direction. Most bass rustlers categorize tackle trays according to lure types—topwater here, diving crank- and swimming-type plugs there, spinnerbaits, jigs, soft plastics, and so on to the tangled bottom of castaways.

Single lure types can sometimes qualify for both boxes. A topwater chugger emphasizes sound, but a stick-type jerk bait relies on sight. Both are surface lures, but one is heavy and creates bold surface displacement, while the other skates and slides with minimal commotion. Similarly, a stubby crankbait with a large, wide lip makes strong vibes as it dives with a tight, fast flutter, yet an elongated "thin minnow" floater/diver with a short lip uses a lazy, rolling, seductive flash to do the job—more image than vibration.

The question, therefore, is not so much whether to go with a crankbait or a topwater lure, but what *kind* of crankbait or topwater? Many anglers simply grab for a recommended lure without realizing that significant differences can exist within the same categories of lure.

It's a difficult call to make. As a general rule, lures that attract by sight are favored under conditions of high visibility—clear water, bright overhead sun, lack of subsurface cover, and lack of wind. Bright, calm, open water is a tough draw. Frankly, that's a lousy day and a lousy spot for catching bass. You might be better off golfing.

But since you are perched in a bass boat, you might as well go for it. Make long casts with lighter line and smaller lures. Show the fish something that looks natural and easy under magnified scrutiny and try not to telegraph your presence.

Sight lures are also effective when working a tightly defined area such as a brushpile weedbed pocket. The bass, within close quarters, will be easy to attract with a slow and appealing offering. In fact, the sudden crash of a pointblank noisemaker might spook the fish. Even a reflexive striker usually requires a moment to sense the approach. Chicken Little and sow bass share a dislike for the sky falling without warning.

Plastic worms, lizards, and jig-eels are classic sight-type offerings for bass in close quarters. The lazy bottom-bumper creates little disturbance and must be worked methodically to create a lingering and taunting temptation.

ON A HIGH-VISIBILITY day the "strike zone" may tighten considerably and force the angler armed with a worm or jig to go inside the perimeter of cover to reach a shaded side if possible. Bass must be coaxed. This is demanding fishing in which a close image is often more successful than a passing noise.

Poor visibility favors sound. Factors of reduced visibility include murky water, thick subsurface vegetation, heavy cloud cover, low sun angle, and a riffled or choppy surface. These conditions, which reduce light penetration, are ideal for bass fishing. The fish are confident and aggressive, which opens the strike zone considerably, from tight feet to generous yards. The bass become headhunters, and a noisy, erratic retrieve is a great way to stir up the weedbeds.

Usually, a faster retrieve complements a noisy lure; however, even at high speed, an erratic stop-and-go motion is the best choice for triggering strikes from following bass. The pauses impart a crippled helplessness that appeals greatly to the largemouth's nature. Nobody ever said we were dealing with a noble and fair-minded fish—just an exciting one.

Motion and commotion are also important factors when covering random water. The slow, methodical image of a worm or jig, though deadly on a defined structure, simply takes too much

Eye-catching lures like these are just the thing to get bass into trouble—but only if the bass can see what you're offering them.

time to fish out along a meandering shoreline or across a vast weedbed. The low profile might pass unnoticed several yards from a receptive fish. The choice would be a vibrating crankbait or spinnerbait, something that reaches out and transmits strong signals to scattered bass.

Ways of making sound are not limited to lure design or action. The caster can excite an aggressive bass with the *plunk* of a falling lure (assuming it isn't dropped right on the fish's head or, worse, tail). Bumping and shaking subsurface cover with the lure during the retrieve is an excellent ploy amid thick tangles. A good example is slow-rolling a big-bladed spinnerbait through a brushtop or over a logjam. The lure batters against the limbs, transmits flurries of nervous vibrations, then flutters enticingly on the drop. Mercenary bass just love this. Using a deep-diving crankbait to bounce and furrow along a shallow bottom is another method of adding to the retrieve. The plowing, grinding crankbait suddenly stops. *Hung,* you think. Then, *Whoa, the snag is moving!* Big bass waxing fat on crawfish are vulnerable to this technique.

Last summer, a friend and I opened the morning by drifting an open, submerged weed flat. The early sky was overcast. He selected a fast-moving, swimming bait and I used a buzz-type spinner-bait—lures that cover water and pump vibrations to prowling bass. We banged several good fish during the first hour and figured we had an effective pattern going; then the

sun broke out and the surface turned to glass. The fish stopped hitting.

The broad flat still suggested fish-finding noisemakers, but the conditions had shifted from low visibility to high visibility. We switched to short 4-inch worms and started tickling the random pockets and edges, hoping to tempt sullen fish with close, easy offerings. It was tedious duty with few defined targets but we landed eight or ten more bass before the midday sun drove us to the dock.

The angler who is tuned in to sight and sound can use one to complement the other. Serving a change-up pitch is a fine way to draw a strike from a previously raised fish. Keep in mind that by switching, you are pushing an entirely different set of buttons. You are offering a new temptation to excite a fresh reaction.

Recently, I burned the lip of a brushpile lunker with a large, double-bladed spinnerbait. The copper willowleaf blades were "waking," stirring the murky surface with a fluttering wobble. As the pulsing lure passed the brush top, the fish rolled up and smacked the lure. The line jerked to the side and, despite a heroic hookset, I fanned air with a "swing and a miss."

Aghast, I marked the location and continued fishing down the shoreline. Two hours later I eased back and lobbed a black plastic lizard into the fish's tangled condominium. The bite was sudden and strong. The rod doubled and a 7-pound sow surged to the surface.

I am confident it was the same fish, and that the switch from a sound to a sight lure was the correct move. Going back with another noisemaker might have discouraged the bass by reminding it of the earlier response. The sight of the quiet, close lizard was a fresh stimulus. No one can say for certain what causes a bass to react, but I do know that the fish was on the lizard as soon as the silent lure dropped.

This business of sight and sound may be an oversimplification, and a lot of gray area exists on most lakes and ponds. Usually, a strike is the result of a combination of sight and sound, but it is seldom a 50/50 split. Depending on the circumstances, one of the two elements takes priority. The difference may be subtle, but it is the trigger. Use it.

By Cliff Hauptman

Some Like It STOPPED

WHEN BASS AREN'T IN
THE MOOD TO EAT ON
THE RUN, OFFER THEM
AN IRRESISTIBLE
MOTIONLESS
MEAL.

I WAS FISHING WITH MY
daughter from our boat, drifting just off the edge of a broad expanse
of lily pads. In an attempt to seduce some fat
yellow perch, Molly was floating a live worm
below a little red-and-white bobber. I was work-

ing the weedy edges with a floating lure that I had been casting out and burbling back across the surface for the past 15 minutes with not even a bump from an interested bass.

Suddenly, Molly's bobber disappeared. So I set down my tackle, leaving the lure to sit neglected out near the weeds. Molly played and landed the perch. I helped her release it and rebait the hook. She cast the rig back out, and I watched to see that she was all set again. Then, before I had a chance to pick up my own rod, my long-immobile lure disappeared in a swirl the size of a manhole cover. Unfortunately, I wasn't ready. But the event did remind me that bass often prefer a lure sitting still to one they have to chase.

Think back to your own fishing experiences. How many times have you tossed out a floating lure, retrieved it a few feet, and than paused to take a bite of a sandwich or a sip of soda, only to have a fish slam the lure as it sat stone still? Or think about those times you've spent tossing a crankbait along the weeds. You cast the lure out and reeled it in a half-dozen times to no avail. Then you backlashed your reel, and while you were picking out the rat's nest, a big bass pounced on the immobile lure like a falcon on a sitting duck. Those events were no accidents. Bass respond extremely well to motionless lures.

As is so often the case in fishing, physiology can speak volumes. Simply taking a good look at the fish we are trying to catch can give us important insight into how best to go about catching it. Look first at a pike or pickerel, for example. It has a wide, flat mouth and comparatively big teeth. The fish is built for flat-out speed with its torpedolike body. Pike and pickerel are best suited for chasing down fast-moving prey and grabbing it in their jaws. Bass, on the other hand, have huge, cavernous mouths. Their bodies are broad-sided and compact. They are built for short bursts and fast turns. They catch their prey not by biting but by opening their mouths, creating an enormous suction that draws their prey along with a lot of water into the cavity, and then blowing the water out their gill flaps while swallowing the food. Clearly, then, while bass are certainly capable

of snatching their prey on the run, they are particularly suited to seizing it while the hapless creature thinks it is siting a safe distance from danger. Surprise!

Surface lures have long been the favorites of bass fishermen because they can be left to sit unmoving for as long as necessary. If there is no wind, the only limit to a lure's sitting-still time is the angler's own patience. Ideally, a floating lure should be cast out and allowed to sit motionless for about 15 seconds. The initial disturbance of the lure's landing can have two opposing effects on bass, depending on where the lure splashes down. If the lure happens to land close to a fish, catching it unaware, it can scare the fish away momentarily, in which case it takes about 15 seconds for the bass to lose its fear and take an interest in seeing what the heck intruded on its solitude. If the lure lands far enough away to avert alarm, it can still take about 15 seconds for the bass to approach it and decide what to do about it.

After that preliminary waiting period, activate the lure briefly. If it is a stickbait, give it about four, good back-and-forth bobs. For a popper or other type of noisemaker, about a foot of commotion will suffice. This action will accomplish two things: It will assure any bass watching the lure that it is alive and worthy of being eaten, and it will further advertise the lure to bass that are not yet aware of its presence. In the former case, it may also spook the fish again, so you must be sure to follow this movement with another period of absolute rest. That will also give incoming bass that are homing in on the noise of the commotion a chance to get there before you snatch it away again.

If there are interested bass in the area, your lure will often be sucked in during this second period of rest, so it is important to develop the patience to let it sit there until you can hear your nerve endings hum. Most often, however, the hit will come the moment you begin to move the lure again after this resting period. Remember, though, that the likelihood of getting that hit depends on the period of motionlessness that precedes it. Don't be too eager to get the lure into motion again.

Time and again I have proven that principle

to myself by varying the waiting time before moving a lure. An experienced angler often can tell that a bass is studying his lure by the subtle bulge in the water the fish makes as it reacts to the lure's movement. On several occasions I have noticed a bass under my lure, and by moving the lure after only brief rests, kept the fish's interest but failed to draw a strike. But when I lengthened the resting interval to the point where I couldn't bear it any longer (usually somewhere around a minute), the fish would smash the lure the instant it moved.

Halting a lure's motion does not apply only to topwater designs. Those types of plugs are the most fun because they stay on the surface and you get to see what is often a spectacular and gut-clenching take. But jigs, spoons, spinners, diving crankbaits, and other subsurface lures appeal to the same instincts in bass. Just because a lure falls through the water when you stop cranking doesn't mean it loses its appeal. In fact, it almost always gains allure immeasurably to an interested bass, even though it has disappeared from your view.

All predators, including bass, instinctively take advantage of the weak and lame. By so doing, they save themselves the costly energy expense of a long chase. Most subsurface lures are endowed with an off-kilter action that imitates a wounded or otherwise imperfect prey. That will often attract the interest of hungry bass, but if the fish are not thoroughly intent on eating, they may still pass up a constantly moving meal. Stop the forward progress of that lure even for a moment, however, and a bass is likely to be on it instantly. So the slower the stopped lure falls through the water, the more effective it will be. Always, especially when fishing soft-plastic jigs, tube lures, and plastic worms, use the least additional weight the conditions will allow. Conversely, when choosing floating/diving crankbaits, which swim underwater but float back to the surface when you stop cranking, favor the ones that rise slowly to the surface when stopped or, better yet, that hang suspended; avoid the ones that pop to the surface like a cork. You want even your subsurface lures to stay nearly still for as long as possible.

Like every good rule, this one has its exceptions. There are situations when it is imperative to keep your lure moving and not stop it at all. Such instances occur when the bass cannot see the lure and are tracking it only by sound. If you are skipping a weedless spoon, frog lure, unweighted Texas-rigged plastic worm, or other similar lure over a dense patch of lily pads, for example, the bass lying below will be reacting purely to the sound of the lure above. If you stop cranking, the bass have no way of knowing where it is. Even if a bass strikes and misses, you must keep retrieving in order to let him have another shot. The same rationale applies to fishing at night.

We all dream of those days when the action is fast and furious, when a lure can be cast out and burned back, and the V-wakes come lancing in like torpedoes to smash our offerings. Some days turn out to be like that. And some species of fish react that way most of the time. But bass more often require subtler handling. They like the teasing, slow roll of a barely turning spinnerbait or the wide, lethargic wiggle of a lazily swimming crankbait. Once you've shown them the seductive qualities of which the lure is capable, however, some—perhaps most—like it stopped.

By Mark Hicks

SPINNING
for Bass

INCREASINGLY, ANGLERS ARE TRADING THEIR BAIT-CASTING GEAR FOR MORE EFFECTIVE LIGHT-LINE TACTICS.

ASS AND BAIT-CASTING HAVE LONG been synonymous, but serious anglers now use spinning tackle more than ever. The transformation is due mainly to light-line tactics that have been proven effective on timid, overfished bass, and in clear lakes where the fish routinely shun big lures and thick lines. Spinning outfits easily handle lightweight offerings and gossamer lines that are extremely difficult to use with bait-casting gear.

While 10-pound-test is considered light for bait-casting, it's regarded as heavy stuff for subtle spinning applications and is usually reserved for fishing near cover. In open, clear water, 6- or 8-pound line does a better job of serving up diminutive lures. Some spinning addicts occasionally drop to 4-pound-test for especially temperamental fish, but this is risky.

Bass are less likely to see and be put off by thin lines, particularly if you stick with clear line or some of the many low-visibility colors currently available. When fished deep, fine line slices through the water, allowing lures to sink faster. It also reduces line bagging, providing better control over the lure and increasing your ability to sense a strike and set the hook.

Because most finesse bass lures are rigged with a single hook, true ultra-light and light-action spinning rods lack sufficient stiffness for consistently

embedding the barb. A medium-action rod rated for 6- to 12- or even 3- to 20-pound line should have the backbone needed to ensure solid hookups. A quality, sensitive graphite rod with a fast tip is well worth the additional expense.

A 6-foot rod is an excellent choice for its versatility. Some anglers like 6½-footers for fishing deep, because long rods take up more line when you set the hook. Others prefer short rods in the 5- to 5½-foot range for improved casting accuracy in tight quarters, such as flooded timber or boat docks.

These areas are just a few of the places where the plastic tube, a lure that is currently taking finicky bass across the country, can be used to advantage. Tubes are hollow, soft plastic cylinders with a blunt, closed-in front and an open-ended back cut into many fine strands for nearly half the length of the lure. The most popular size for bass measures just under 4 inches long and ½ inch in diameter. You can hide a jig inside the tube by slipping the leadhead in from the back, pushing it to the front, and poking the line eye through the plastic.

A tube with a 1/16-ounce jig sinks with a slow, wavering action that bass find irresistible. It's an excellent combination for wary fish that are found near flooded timber, boat docks, and just about any shallow cover in clear water. Leave the hook exposed whenever possible. If snagging is a problem, use one of several tube-jig designs that feature hook guards.

Don't try to penetrate cover when fishing tubes with light line. The trick is to cast to the edge of objects and draw bass out. Some anglers skip tubes over the surface, a ploy that resembles a fleeing baitfish. Skipping also lets you get tubes far under boat docks and other targets that are inaccessible with conventional casting. Note that although skipping is performed easily with spinning tackle, it is a backlash nightmare for bait-casting. Many strikes come moments after the tube skitters to a halt and begins its tantalizing fall. When a strike occurs, let the bass swim away from the cover toward deeper water before setting the hook.

SWIMMING A TUBE also triggers strikes from reluctant bass. Simply let the lure sink to the desired depth, hold the rod tip at about 10 o'clock, and maintain a slow, steady cranking. This will draw largemouths and smallmouths from many types of cover. One excellent place to swim tubes for largemouth and smallmouth bass is over the edges of submerged weeds that are visible beneath the surface, but the tube's effectiveness isn't limited to shallow water. When matched with heavier jigs weighing up to 3/8 ounce, it readily takes largemouth, spotted, and smallmouth bass from depths up to 50 feet. The combination is being used regularly in rocky canyon and highland reservoirs that have crystalline water, and in some regions of the Great Lakes.

With the swimming retrieve, the tube mimics a minnow; this calls for baitfish colors such as

Sweepset with Light Line

The most common problem bass anglers experience when they first take up light-line spinning is breaking off while setting the hook. This is especially prevalent among those who cut their teeth on stiff bait-casting rods, stout line, and the "cross their eyes" mentality.

Adjust the spinning reel's drag to roughly 50 percent of the line strength, so that it has enough resistance for hook-setting, yet will give line before breaking it. When a bass strikes, cool your jets and resist the urge to snap the rod up with everything you can muster. Instead, use the sweepset. Drop the rod tip slightly, take up the slack, and sweep the rod up firmly until you feel the weight of the bass. Then simply maintain steady pressure.

The sweepset usually jabs the hook's point into the fish, and the fish's resistance actually sinks the barb. Never use a hook that isn't sharp enough to dig into your thumbnail at the slightest touch. If you lack the ability to hand-hone hooks to this degree of sharpness, there are a few electric hook sharpeners on the market that do an excellent job.

Worms in Weed Pockets

When you cast a plastic worm into a weed pocket with spinning tackle, the line flows freely from the spool and lets the lure sink all the way to the bottom.

The resistance caused by a bait-casting reel makes the worm drift toward the angler, which often prevents the lure from getting down to the bass.

clear sparkle, chartreuse sparkle, salt and pepper, and other light hues. When hopping a tube over the bottom like a crayfish, go with darker colors, such as pumpkin, motor oil/red sparkle, smoke/red sparkle, and brown salt and pepper.

These colors are also deadly with 3- to 5-inch fat grubs, which work well with light spinning tackle. Fat grubs have very wide, nimble ribbon tails, and they are most often fished with open jig hooks. They do most of their damage from the middle depths to deep water, and over rocky or clean bottoms. Both swimming and bottom-hopping retrieves are effective.

Fat grubs are one of several lures now being used with a light-line method called split-shotting. The grub is rigged on a size 1 or 1/0 worm hook, preferably with the point exposed. When snags are a possibility, push the point just under the skin of the plastic to ensure that it will pop free when the hook is set. A single large split shot, such as a No. 4, is clamped onto the line about 18 inches above the hook. This lets the lure swim with a freer, more natural motion, whether you are dragging bottom or swimming the rig over submerged points and similar structures. Other lures that work well with split shot are reapers, which have flat tails that make them glide through the water, and skinny, 4-inch worms.

A thin, straight 4-inch worm is the heart of the doodling system, which is acclaimed by many anglers who fish deep, clear bass waters.

Rig the rod with 6-pound-test, and then thread the line through a 3/16-ounce slip-sinker, followed by an 8mm glass bead. Tie on a size 1/0 worm hook and rig it Texas-style so the hook point lies inside the plastic. Peg the worm by pushing a strand of 50-pound-test monofilament through the head of the lure and the eye of the hook. Clip off the excess line.

Doodling involves shaking the rod tip during the retrieve, which causes the slip-sinker to rattle against the glass bead. Proponents claim this *tic-tic-tic* sound imitates the sound made by crayfish and goads bass into striking. Pegging the worm prevents it from sliding down the hook while you're shaking the rod or when bass tug on the tail, which they do often.

When you feel bass tugging but can't seem to hook them, continue shaking and try not to set the hook until you sense the steady weight that indicates a bass has fully engulfed the worm. It will take practice to get the timing down. Doodling pays off especially well when you find bass suspended along bluff banks, over points, humps, and other structures, and when they are hugging bottom in deep water.

For suspended fish, cast out, count the worm down to the proper depth—approximately 1 foot per second—and then swim the lure back at that depth while shaking the rod tip. If the fish are deeper than 25 feet or so, put the boat directly over them, measure the line out 1 foot at a time to the desired depth, and commence shaking. When bass are on the bottom, go with the drag-shake. After the worm hits the bottom, simultaneously drag and shake it. When you lose contact with the bottom, pause, let the worm fall back, and continue drag-shaking.

My friend Larry Williams has mastered most of these light-line methods, and he also relies on spinning tackle when fishing stronger lines in heavy cover. A four-time Bassmasters Classic qualifier, Williams uses spinning reels that have large diameter spools almost exclusively and the same stout 6½- to 7½-foot rod blanks normally reserved for bait-casting. He uses 12- to 17-pound-test line and has little trouble extracting sizable bass from dense weeds, bushes, and other cover.

Spinning reels allow Williams to accurately cast lightweight offerings on substantial line to bass holding in cover, something that is almost impossible to do with bait-casting. His favorite lure is a 4-inch worm with a 1/16-ounce slip sinker. Williams is convinced that finesse lures are often needed to encourage strikes from bass hiding in cover, and it's hard to argue with his success.

The heavy spinning gear also lets him skip weedless spoons and plastic worms into tight spots. He claims that spinning is unequaled for fishing plastic worms in weedbeds, because the line feeds freely off the spool after the cast, allowing the worm to drop straight down to the bottom of holes and openings. The line resistance caused by a bait-casting reel makes the worm drift toward the angler, preventing it from ever getting down to the bass.

The popularity of spinning for bass is likely to grow in the years ahead. With more fishing pressure and increasingly wary bass, spinning tackle and finesse methods are becoming a prerequisite for consistent bass fishing success.

How to Skip a Tube

Hold the rod tip low and make a sharp cast at the water's surface several feet in front of your target (1). The tube will bounce over the surface several times, covering a distance of 10 feet or more. If it touches down unmolested (2), jump it up sharply, and let it drop back to the bottom (3). After three or four jumps, crank in quickly and cast to another object.

By Joe Doggett

TALKING TRASH

CHEAP SHOTS WITH BANANA-SIZED
TOPWATER PLUGS WILL GOAD ANY
SELF-RESPECTING
LARGEMOUTH INTO
A SPECTACULAR STRIKE.

A BIG BASS SLICED A
bulging arc against the grassy
shoreline. The sudden wake terminated
in a heaving splash. The fish swapped ends, buck-
ling the water, and plowed back to its mossy lair.
The attack probably claimed a small sunfish.

And it certainly pointed to a big opportunity. I had just been handed the location of a hungry and receptive bass.

Sadly, I greeted this charity with an overflight. The topwater plug sailed beyond the rim of open water and impacted amid the reeds. I slumped. *All I'd needed to do was hit the water.*

The surface against the vegetation stirred. The bass was there, aroused by the disturbance and sensing fresh opportunity for mayhem. I twiggled the rod, hoping to flip the lure free, and succeeded in snagging an unseen branch. The line ran tight and unyielding. The near water bulged with pressing interest.

Frustrated with the standoff, I started yanking. The brittle twig broke, splatting the water as the freed lure skittered across the surface. The waiting bass pounded the plug, wrenching the rod against a startled hookset.

I'll take credit for the 5-pounder, but it was a cheap shot. It also was a bold example, albeit an unintentional one, of talking trash with a topwater plug.

THE "TOP" WAY to trigger a violent disruption is to agitate and irritate a bass. Yank his chain. A bass feeling secure amid the shadowed haunts of weeds and brush can be challenged into striking. The amount and volume of noise are not as important as the message. You can talk trash with a large, angry lure, clattering and chugging and gouging, or you can taunt and tease with a small, reserved bait, flipping and twitching and mocking.

The amount of commotion may depend on circumstance, with the heavier hand usually favoring conditions of reduced visibility such as murky water, low-angle light, or surface chop. Even depth can be a factor. Loud or soft, you are sneering, *Here I am and I'm dancing right over your head. Come on! Hit me with your best shot!*

The largemouth bass is a swashbuckler. A revved-up bass can be teased until it rises to the occasion—and this "rise" is an emphatic blast that rates among the finest in fishing.

Pound-for-pound, few fish pushing freshwater can match the surface strike of the largemouth. The "bass-o profundo," with its wide and hollow maw combined with large and flaring gill plates, creates an impressive expulsion of water and air. The assault of this topwater terrorist is out of proportion to the size of the fish. The largemouth has the biggest hit in North America. Some anglers above the Mason-Dixon line may argue in favor of pike or muskellunge. No doubt, an agitated muskie swarming after a mallard duck can make a glorious commotion, but remember the pound-for-pound factor. Slip a 40-pound mutated largemouth into the same weedbed and you will admit that, yes, the bass makes a bigger splash when it eats the muskie.

It is this voracious attitude that makes the normal 2- to 5-pound bass such a marvelous antagonist on the surface. Should the exceptional 8-pounder churn into the fray, sparks seem to fly with the spray. This is a fish—a moment—that truly is larger than life.

You may feel strange trying to slap a fish in the face with an outrageous plug the size of a banana, but this is no time to be tentative. To reiterate, you are not attempting to imitate a meek and fearful prey. Your task is to torment Brother Bass, to make his fins bristle and his scales glow and maybe his eyes bulge a bit. I'm not kidding. An irritated largemouth seems to possess a terrible core energy. If you've ever seen a bass in this condition up close, you immediately are thankful they don't grow to 6 or 8 feet in length. Welcome to Jurassic Pond.

There certainly is nothing new about the concept of challenging a bigmouth. Generations ago, savvy swamp fishermen used long cane poles rigged with short lengths of heavy line and large spinner/feather lures. The boater armed with a sculling paddle and a "jiggerpole" would slip into position and churn and sweep the lure repeatedly across the surface until resident bass were goaded into striking. These rigs were so effective they were outlawed in some areas.

The angler armed with conventional high-tech casting tackle is, frankly, less prepared to talk trash than his forebear wielding the long pole. The level-winder lacks the vertical presentation of the jiggerpoler. He might be able to cast over rimming surface cover to reach a pocket, but he cannot extract the lure without retrieving through the rough. Nor can he keep a lure fussing back and forth through the same tight strike zone to taunt a lurking fish. In short, he is not as efficient.

Still, with accurate and repeated casts he can push enough bass to the boiling point to make the technique well worthwhile. The serious student follows the lead of the past and leans heavily on plugs rigged with spinners, or propellers. The slushing and capering of the flashing blades have a knack of twisting even indifferent bass. Considering the effectiveness of twirling blades, the so-called buzz spinners and standard safety-pin spinners can talk an effective, if unorthodox, brand of trash. The straight paddling whir of a buzzbait chunked repeatedly into a pocket or along a weedline can incite strikes even under the high sun—a trump that more pluggers discouraged by the traditional midday topwater slump might consider.

The snagless safety-pin spinner can be dredged on or just below the surface, "waking" through likely haunts such as stickups and brushpiles. If the clattering lure bumps and batters the limbs or stalks, so much the better. The riot of vibrations helps excite lurking bass.

With plugs or spinnerbaits, repeated casts to the same spot can light a slow burn in the weedbeds. The hits are dramatic and the fish often are large. Bass with shoulders are, after all, the ones most apt to respond to a brazen challenge.

Given these potbellied possibilities, if you attempt to talk trash, you'd best be able to back it up. A stiff rod butt, a heavy casting line, and a lure with no-nonsense hooks and riggings are prerequisites. Most of this bullying will occur over and near dreadful tangles of subsurface cover. A big bass raging up and swapping ends will dig hard for limbs and moss; this power dive may be short but it can put great and sudden stress on tackle. Remember, this bass is "runnin' hot." This is a different fish than the bass that cozies up and leisurely inhales a soft-plastic bottom-bumper. The worm bass is on a more-or-less level plane, and you have a moment or two to turn the startled fish and start it to the surface. When a big sow slam-dunks a topwater plug, everything's going the other way as you raise the rod.

The importance of adequate tackle cannot be overemphasized. A rod with guts can ram the heavy hooks home and discourage that first thrust to cover. The casting line should be as heavy as you can get away with; at least 15-pound-test, up to 25 or 30 if conditions permit. Visibility seldom is an issue; the topwater retrieve keeps most of the line above the water and the jiving pace creates sufficient surface disturbance to obscure the terminal connection.

The natural reaction on a loud, splashy strike is to rear back with a full-house yank. Such "eye-crossing" heroics may not be necessary; worse, a mighty heave-ho can be dangerous, sizzling the heavy plug and gleaming hooks back in your face. The longer I fish, the more convinced I become that a short-arc tip set is all that is necessary to hook the typical topwater strike. The main-line contact from rod tip to fish reduces the line-stretch factor, and if the points are sharp and the rod has authority, the combination of a firm wrist-snap against the straight resistance should engage the hooks.

A miss bounces the lure only a few feet, keeping it within the strike zone of the aggressive bass. Unless you burned a lip with the hooks, the prospects are excellent for a prompt follow-up grab. The mighty yank forfeits this immediate play. Even the most determined bass might have trouble claiming a plug swinging from a line or dangling from an earlobe.

Assuming that the bass grabs the lure, few if any points are lost during a slight delay on the hookset. I just don't buy the old wisdom that a lightning-fast yank is critical with a topwater strike; frankly, a hair trigger might snatch the lure from a fish doing its best to get caught.

The concept of challenging bass goes against established concepts of coy deception and subtle presentation. I am not suggesting that gentle twitches and lingering pauses are not effective; indeed, a softer touch can be deadly on skittish or sluggish fish. But bass have weird mood shifts. Remember, this is a headhunter that will attack a water moccasin or a baby alligator, a big-mouthed, potbellied predator that couldn't care less about No. 22 emerger nymphs. Respect this mean side. When the soft touch gets boring, take a deep breath and a firm grip and start talking trash.

Fin's Bass Jig

When Phineas "Fin" Graham retired and moved South to Georgia's Lake Seminole, he became frustrated by the big largemouths he knew were holed up beneath the dense hydrilla that covered the water's surface. The flipping rod and lures he normally used to overcome such heavy cover were rendered useless, and Fin set out to find a way through this barrier.

The solution came to him when he found a mold for an egg-shaped 1⅛-ounce spinnerbait head. Fin molded a head around a straight, removable wire in place of a spinnerbait hook and wireform. He painted his creation a glittering metal-flake color and fitted the collar with a matching silicone skirt. He threaded his line through the center of the weight and tied it to a 6/0 worm hook dressed with a 4-inch plastic crayfish. The concoction resembled a typical bass jig, but the heft and smooth oval shape of the head allowed it to slither through the dense weed mats.

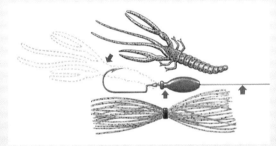

"The second time I pitched the lure into the hydrilla, I hooked a bass that immediately broke my 17-pound line," recalled Fin. "I moved up to 25-pound-test and managed to horse the next one out—a 5-pounder."

The episode was a proper initiation for a lure that has since become a regular around Jack Wingate's Lunker Lodge, Fin's regular hangout. Troy Barfield, a guide who's been fishing Seminole for more than fifteen years, is especially high on Fin's jig.

"I catch bass on that thing all year long," he says. "The best time is right in the middle of the summer when the hydrilla mats get so thick in places that the alligators can lay on top of them without sinking through."

During the hot months, Barfield catches his biggest bass from the hydrilla beds near the deep river channels on the main lake. He positions his boat close to the outer edges of the weed-beds, and flips or pitches Fin's jig on top of the carpet, 5 to 30 feet away. If the lure stays on the grass, he'll jiggle the rod tip until it breaks through. To penetrate especially thick mats, Barfield tosses the lure up, about 8 feet high, and lets its weight plunge it down into the vegetation. Once the jig pops through, it's readily visible to bass holding in the more open water below.

Barfield works the lure up and down a few times just beneath the mat, because many strikes come within 2 feet of the surface. When bass are less aggressive, he lets Fin's jig sink to the bottom, which is 3 to 15 feet deep. He'll jig the lure a few more times and then hit the next spot. The idea is to work fast until you start getting bites; then slow down and fish thoroughly.—*Mark Hicks*

By Doug Pike

TWEAKING LURES

SAME WATER, SAME TECHNIQUE, SAME LURE.
DRAMATICALLY DIFFERENT RESULTS.
OR SO IT HAS SEEMED ON OCCASIONS
WHEN I'VE BEEN ON THE SHORT END OF
THAT MOST FRUSTRATING STICK.

YOU KNOW THE SCEN-ario. A partner's lure gathers fish after fish, while yours might as well be on a shelf gathering dust.

The question is, "Why?" The answer lies most often in only one of a session's three basic elements. It can't be the water; no one is capable of manipulating rivers and oceans on a whim. And it probably isn't technique; study someone else's retrieve once or twice, and a fisherman of even modest ability can come pretty close to replicating it.

Which leaves the lure.

Every artificial lure started as a concept, a fanciful blend of engineering and creativity hoped to set that one bait apart from all the others. A model was built by hand from plastic

or wood or metal, tests were conducted, and a finely tuned, new, and (hopefully) better fishing lure found its way into tackle boxes.

It isn't in the nature of fishermen, though, to leave well enough alone—especially fishing lures. As if we didn't have enough styles, colors, sizes, and shapes to befuddle us already, fishermen armed with pocket tools, a little hardware, and a paintbrush can generate an infinite number of variations on any theme.

Of course, most of the artficials on tackle store shelves today are simply resurrected classics doctored to suit contemporary tastes. The same big fish have eaten the same little fish for centuries, after all. The evolution of lures has not been so much in design as it has in materials, manufacturing processes, and finishing techniques.

My first introduction to the art of fine-tuning came years ago on Lake Conroe, just north of Houston. Former NFL punter Jerrel Wilson was doing a little guiding and a lot of work as owner of a marina. There came a day when he needed a break from both and asked me to join him on a bass fishing trip.

The surface was unusually calm for a lake on which mostly bulkheaded shorelines— thanks to incessant resort development—cause

wind chop to rebound rather than dissipate, and the thick, overcast sky never made good on its threat of showers. With the trolling motor dialed to its lowest speed, Wilson worked the boat methodically along a rocky breakwater. His Pop-R surface plug and mine were twins plucked from the same pegboard hook in Wilson's store. Each had silver sides, a bright blue back, and a splash of white bucktail hiding the rear treble. Wilson's caught fish. Lots of fish. Mine did not.

After letting me fall several fish behind, Wilson confessed to having made a subtle change in his lure just before we left the dock that caused it to skip and spit rather than splash and chug. With a small pocket knife, he'd carefully sliced away the bluntness of the lure's lower lip. On slick water, he said, surface plugs that made too much commotion tended to spook more bass than they attracted.

My friend Gene Ballard, a full-time pro basser from Fayetteville, Texas, laughed at the story of Wilson's trickery.

"I do the same thing to my Pop-R's for calm water," Ballard said. "Only I like to scrape mine down on concrete instead of using a knife—leaves a little smoother edge."

I confessed my surprise and told him I'd always thought that once you sharpened or replaced the hooks, a new lure was supposed to be "good to go" right out of the box.

Ballard laughed at my innocence.

"Crankbaits are a real problem," he said. "Only about one or two in a dozen runs 'true' from the factory. But a lot of people don't realize you can adjust them, and some of those who do don't know how to do it right."

The mechanics are simple. A crankbait's lip causes it to dive, and its reversed-teardrop shape triggers that spirited wiggle, much like that of a kite with no tail. Those are the big things. The littlest thing on a crankbait, its eye, determines whether the bait tracks straight or wants to veer to port or starboard.

"You don't want to twist the eye like you're unscrewing it," Ballard said. "You have to physically bend it, very gently to the left or right, with a needlenosed plier. It only takes a little, too; most times, you'll overcorrect."

He also cautioned that since the jaws of pointed pliers are typically grooved or roughed to provide more secure purchase, they can nick the lure's delicate eye, which is sure to damage monofilament and result in unexplained breakoffs. To protect the lure, either cover the plier jaws with heavy tape or slip the hem of a T-shirt between tool and tie eye.

Ballard solved a years-long problem on his home lake, Fayette County Reservoir, by tinkering with yet another topwater plug.

"We get some really wild schooling bass action here in late summer," he explained. "Fish up to 5 or 6 pounds are blowing up on shad all over the lake, and they'll knock the fire out of a lure if you can get it in there while the fish are up. When the wind doesn't blow and you can see the schools, a couple of fishermen who know what they're doing can get a lot of big bass in a day."

Until recently, the favored lure here was one of two baits, the Boy Howdy or the Zara Puppy (a pint-sized version of the Zara Spook), but both had limitations. The former was considerably longer than the juvenile shad on which these bass feed, and the latter was too light to be cast far enough to intercept breaking schools.

"I tried Tiny Torpedoes because they're a little heavier but about the right size and shape," Ballard said. "They did okay, but they weren't getting as many bites as the other baits."

One afternoon in his boat shed, Ballard disassembled a Tiny Torpedo and removed its rear propeller, essentially rendering it a "slush bait" with no slush.

"I really hate for you to write anything about it," Ballard said. "I can reach schools now that would have been way out of range with the Puppy. Late last summer, I slayed the fish on that thing. Even had six or seven doubles, one hanging from the front hook and another on the back hook. It's made all the difference in the world. There was just something they didn't like about slush baits, and I knew I had to make some kind of adjustment. Taking that propeller off was what it took to get the most out of the lure."

Another good idea for all top-water baits, Ballard said, is to add a small split ring, which frees the lure to move side-to-side more than when line is tied directly to the eye. Loop knots are a lazy man's shortcut to the same action but put unnecessary stress on the fishing line.

Spinnerbaits and buzzbaits seem pretty cut-and-dried, but look again. They're a tinkerer's dream. Both come with easily removed parts—blades and skirts—that just beg to be switched and swapped.

When it comes to tinkering and tweaking, though, nobody outdoes the fishing tournament pros, who will go to great lengths to gain a competitive edge.

"I know guys who'll drive 400 or 500 miles to a tournament, holding their buzzbaits out the window the whole way," Ballard said, explaining that high speed pinwheeling wears the metal on blade and shaft, which creates a

Spinnerbaits and buzzbaits seem pretty cut-and-dried, but they're a tinkerer's dream.

bit of extra play between the two. In the water, the result is a constant, fingernails-down-a-chalkboard squeak in addition to the sputter of the turning blade.

Another way to increase buzzbait noise is to bend the top arm slightly downward so the rotating blade just barely makes contact with the bottom arm. Squeeze too hard, and the blade won't turn. At just the right angle, though, the blade emits an audible *tick* every time it spins across the lure's lower arm.

Spinnerbaits and buzzbaits can also be altered so that they'll run almost parallel to a shoreline or grass bed, which increases time spent in the strike zone. Lures that hug the cover also keep you from having to maneuver the boat right on top of the fish, a tremendous competitive edge. The same alteration works well for bank fishermen, too. Canted just so, a spinnerbait can be thrown 15 or 20 yards to a target 3 feet off the bank, and it will maintain that proximity to the shore until it is nearly back to the rod tip. Holding a lure in both hands, one on the top arm and the other on the bottom, gently pivot the top arm off-center. The more dramatic the resultant angle, the harder the lure will pull away from direct line of retrieve.

You might also want to tinker with the other end of these lures. At times, bass have an annoying habit of shortstriking spinnerbaits and buzzbaits, and the standard quick fix is the addition of a "stinger" or "trailer" hook. Instead, use scissors to trim skirt material so that it barely extends beyond the original hook. The fish will hit that smaller target more squarely, and they're more likely to find the hook when they do.

"Suspending" lures, particularly jerkbaits, were all the rage this spring on Southern lakes; the effectiveness of "neutral buoyancy" was proved time and again in amateur and professional tournaments. Lures in this new family follow their lips to a specific depth, then remain on that plane throughout the retrieve. Some

manufacturers added weights to reach the delicate balance between float and sink; others got results by using water as ballast in hollowed sections of their plugs. And some dedicated tinkerers made their own by altering the flotation of lures already on hand with the trial-and-error addition of thin strips of lead tape.

When soft jerkbaits came onto the bass fishing scene, the term "erratic retrieve" was elevated to a new level. With every twitch of the rod, these nondescript chunks of plastic chart a new course. By the time most recreational fishermen figured out how to work this specialized breed of baits, though, the pros had already discovered ways to make them work even better. By adding a short piece of pliable wire to the nose section and bending it just so, a soft jerkbait can be manipulated to dart primarily in one direction (to hug weed lines or ridges), ride enticingly over surface vegetation without fouling, or bury its nose in the bottom and stir plugs of silt. Under specific circumstances, any of these variations can provide a marked advantage over using the same bait fresh from the package.

A box full of paints and small brushes can inspire unlimited innovation. Lures that don't come with eyes or gills or mouths can obtain them courtesy of a few carefree strokes. Add spots or stripes, or even a paisley print if you like. A bit of advice: Start slowly, and proceed with moderation. I once went through a "lure enhancement" phase that would have left a classroom of kindergarten finger painters giggling uncontrollably. When the paint finally dried, a host of top-quality baits had been reduced to gaudy, ridiculous junk.

Even plastic worms, despite manufacturers' efforts to provide anglers with every conceivable size, shape, and color combination, have not been spared the tinkerer's hand. The simplest and most effective alterations to soft plastics are done with dyes, which Ballard said he considers essential equipment, keeping chartreuse, blue, and red (dyes) on hand at all times. On some worms that feature a contrasting tail color from the manufacturer, that color is opaque. Many of the pros prefer to buy worms that are the same color end to end, then use translucent dyes—which don't mask the original pattern and hue—to alter tails as dictated by conditions. The dip-your-own strategy saves money as well—instead of buying blue/white, blue/chartreuse, and blue/firetail worms, you just buy blue worms and dip a few each trip in the hottest tail color.

But color is only the beginning of the innovation process. Some fishermen go so far as to carry hypodermic syringes and inject their worms with air to increase flotation, and others will take a perfectly good worm and cut it in half.

There are no fast rules that define when a lure should be left alone and when it should be tweaked. Fine-tuning is merely the random adoption of knowledge and imagination to exceptional circumstance. It's instinct, a hunch; it's stopping to wonder, *What if?* Which, by the way, has been the origin of every fishing lure ever made.

By Wade L. Bourne

The Go-
BETWEEN

GETTING AT MID-DEPTH BASS
MEANS USING A LURE WITH THE
RIGHT APPEAL.

ABOVE THE SURFACE, the lake appears as serene as a baby's smile. The face of the water is quiet, broken only by an occasional stroke of wind or a lullaby of waves from a boat long since past.

However, below the surface is a world infinitely more savage. This mix of liquid and murk is marked by terror and quick death. Predator fish stalk unsuspecting prey, rushing from ambush to devour or herd schools of baitfish, until one minnow is injured, triggering an all-out attack and panicked flight.

This life/death drama holds special significance for bass fishermen because most of this activity occurs in an intermediate band of water sandwiched between the shallows and the deep. This in-between range is the aquatic equivalent of a killing field. It is where bass come to feed.

It is also where they can be caught, not exclusively, but most effectively both for numbers and for size, says pro angler Bill Dance of Memphis, Tennessee, who has spent years testing this theory on waters across the country. "Mid-depth bass can be the easiest fish in a lake to catch," he says. "When you find them in this layer, they're there to eat something, so they're active and not too spooky. What's more, they're dependable, feeding in the same places day after day. So if you locate a school, and don't catch too many at one time, you can usually enjoy them for an extended period."

But being in the right place at the right time can be another matter. Dance says, "The first step is to focus on places that border deep water, like steep banks, channel drops, or submerged points. Bass like quick access to deep sanctuaries, and they especially like spots that face into prevailing winds or currents, which wash baitfish to them."

Dance suggests using a lake map and depthfinder to find spots that might attract

John Hope of Palestine, Texas, says the mid-layer is especially important to bass after the spawn ends, because from then until winter that's where most of the foraging occurs.

He should know. Hope is a researcher who has spent the last eight years conducting radio-tracking studies on thirty-three largemouths, ranging in size from 3-pound "chunks" to 15-pound "monsters," in lakes in Texas, Missouri, and Ohio.

Hope says that when bass grow to approximately 7 pounds, they undergo a radical change in behavior. After attaining lunker size, they become loners and spend nonfeeding hours suspended in open water away from structure. They fin to the nearest shoreline or ledge and patrol for food in the in-between depths of 8 to 12 feet, depending

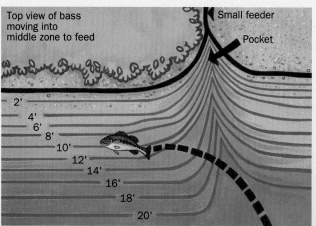

Top view of bass moving into middle zone to feed

Small feeder

Pocket

2'
4'
6'
8'
10'
12'
14'
16'
18'
20'

on water clarity. The clearer the water, the deeper bass feed.

"Many of these big, solitary fish relate to what I call 'funnel areas,' where deep water runs into shallow," says Hope. On a map, these little underwater gullies, draws, and creeks look like notches in the bank. The contour lines run parallel to each other, then suddenly narrow, forming a V that points toward the shoreline.

"My tracking studies have shown that big bass suspend away from these pockets over the closest deep areas. When it's time to feed, they follow these funnels into shore and cruise back and forth around the points and adjacent banks.

"And the tighter the funnel," adds Hope, "the easier it is to catch a fish patrolling it."—W.L.B.

---

feeding bass, such as dropoffs, humps, and points. Then get out on the water, locate, and test-fish these areas, paying special attention to the presence of baitfish. If minnows are concentrated around a place, you can bet that bass are close by.

"Now, conducting this search sounds easy, but it takes a lot of perseverance," says Dance. "You might check ten places before you find a good one, but that one spot will be worth the effort."

The key to your success will be in using the right bait and presentation. Several combinations can stir up action, but crankbaiting, "slow-rolling" spinnerbaits, and dragging Carolina-rigged plastic worms or lizards are the best at imitating the fast-moving targets bass seek out in the middle zone.

Both diving and lipless crankbaits can be

deadly on mid-level bass, but you'll need to experiment with both types of lure to see which one the fish prefer.

Diving crankbaits produce best when rooting along bottom, digging up mud or sand, and careening off rocks or stumps. Be sure to select a crankbait that'll dive deep enough to maintain bottom contact at the depth you're fishing. If you're working an 8-foot contour, for example, use a crankbait that dives to at least 10 feet. This will let you contact the bottom quickly, then crawl the bait over the structure. Sometimes an erratic, stop-and-go retrieve will trigger strikes when a steady pull is being ignored.

Lipless crankbaits offer an entirely different action, and are designed for swimming above the bottom. After a long cast, an angler will count a lipless crankbait down to the desired depth (most models sink approximately 1 foot per second), then steadily reel the bait back in.

When working an 8-foot contour, for instance, a fisherman may count a lipless crankbait down to 5 feet, then swim it back 3 feet off the bottom. These lures work best on long banks, submerged weedlines, and other similar, broad expanses.

Slow-rolling a spinnerbait is a mid-depth adaptation for this typically shallow-water bait. Use a heavy lure of at least ½ ounce, with large Colorado or willowleaf blades. Cast along a contour, engage your reel, and wait until the spinnerbait helicopters to the bottom. Then start a retrieve that's just fast enough to keep the bait running above the bottom structure, in the prime strike zone.

For a "slimy critter" look in a fast-moving presentation try a Carolina-rigged plastic worm or lizard. Rig it with a ½- to 1-ounce sliding weight threaded up the line ahead of a barrel swivel, with a 3- to 5-foot monofilament leader trailing the lure behind. Bury the hook point in the bait or leave it exposed, according to the amount of cover and likelihood of snagging.

When this rig is cast, the weight will pull the bait quickly to the bottom. Reel up slack and begin a steady lift-and-drop retrieve. As the weigh hops along bottom, it emits a tantalizing commotion that many bass can't resist.

While these presentations typically yield the best results on bass between top and bottom, jerkbaits, soft-plastic stickbaits, jigs-and-pigs, and other sinking or diving standbys can also close the deal in this productive area.

Bass fishermen often talk about topwater and bottom-hugging but that leaves a lot of water uncovered. The fact is that bass like to have a few feet of water above and several feet below, or at least close by. According to Dance, catching these fish is simply a matter of finding the right level—and then sending the lure best able to act as a go-between.

Crankbait Considerations

Although diving crankbaits are the top picks for catching bass in the middle levels, this family of lures includes a confusing array of choices. Running depth is the main consideration. Use divers designed to run at mid-depths of 5 to 12 feet. You can tell how deep a lure dives by experimenting, or by reading the instructions on the packaging.

Beyond running depth, however, anglers must decide which shape of lure will best satisfy their particular fishing conditions. There are two choices: fat and flat. Fat-bodied crankbaits have a slow, wide-wobbling action that's best when the bite is hot. This lure's exaggerated action excites feeding fish and triggers impulse strikes. Also, a fat body is the right pick for dingy water, when excessive motion and vibration are needed to attract attention and lead bass to the bait.

Conversely, a flat, thin-bodied crankbait is best when bass are not aggressive and/or when the water clarity is high. Thin crankbaits aren't as obtrusive as their fat counterparts; their appearance and action are more natural and shadlike. Bass turned off by a wide-wobbler will be more likely to strike this baitfish clone.—W.L.B.

By Ken Schultz

The Power of PLASTIC

HOPPING OR CRAWLING ONE OF THESE "WORMS" TOWARD A BASS IN DEEP COVER IS A GOOD WAY TO TRIGGER AN EXPLOSION.

*I*T MAY BE HARD FOR bass fishermen to imagine a world without plastic worms, but in fact the ancestor of what has become the most popular lure in history first appeared in the mid-1950s, when it was made out of rubber and was called Black Magic. In its present soft-plastic, many-colored, many-shaped form, it numbers in the millions, maybe billions, and has probably caught more bass than all other lure types put together. Such is the power of the plastic worm that without it, bass fishing might never have developed into the super sport it is today.

Although plastic worms can be used in a variety of situations, they are particularly valuable for working the bottom in heavy cover, where most conventional bass lures don't come *to* bass, but go *by* them. They cannot work where the fish are without getting hung up. Not so the plastic worm. Slow-moving, unob-

trusive, and virtually snag-free, it goes wherever it has to to catch bass.

With the hook buried in its body, a worm can be maneuvered through all types of cover: the edges of vegetation, including lily pads, moss beds, and milfoil; the branches of trees that have fallen into the water; stumps, especially those with large root systems; standing timber; log and driftwood jams; and bushes and brushpiles.

Worms are also good around sunken objects. This is a broad category of bass habitat involving everything from discharge pipes, dock cribs, and foundations to boats, including sunken rowboats and barges, which can usually be counted on to produce some bass.

Since plastic worms are not very successful in cold water, they are mostly a summer lure, though depending on where you live and when the water warms or cools, they can be productive in spring and fall as well.

They are most often fished during the day, when bass are less venturesome. Actually, plastic worms are just as useful early and late in the day and at night, but in low light conditions, fishermen generally prefer to use fast-moving lures to cover ground and find eager fish. Proper plastic worm fishing is not a run-and-gun activity, as these lures have to be worked in a deliberate manner. When you're fishing with other lures, a plastic worm makes a great second-chance bait. Many anglers carry a

spare rod rigged with a plastic worm so they can toss the worm out immediately after a fish has struck and missed a surface lure, spinnerbait, or crankbait. Bass usually won't strike the same lure if it is tossed back at them, but they will grab the less obtrusive-looking worm. This is especially common with larger fish and around heavy cover.

Worms come in all sizes and many styles. Smaller worms have become very popular recently, especially in heavily fished areas where 4-inch worms on thin line are often used to dupe wary bass. In thick cover use heavier lines and larger worms, in the 6- to 8-inch range, which are more compelling to fish waiting in ambush.

Although most fishermen develop their own personal favorites among the huge variety of plastic worms, no one worm is successful everywhere and at all times. In cold water, for example, you might prefer a flat-tailed worm because it works simply, and bass are more sluggish in cold water. In warm water, where bass are more active, a curly-tailed worm, or even one with two curled tails, that swims in a vibrant enticing manner might be called for.

Worms with active tail designs swim well, but they're tough to use in heavy cover because the tail grabs onto things. A straight-tailed worm clings less and moves better in jungle-like cover.

When fishing in cover, I'm partial to worms with dark bodies that have some added flash or color, such as sparkled flecks or a light tail, because the aquatic conditions are often thick, dark, and/or murky. Worms with two lateral tones, some with partially clear and flecked bodies, are also good for fishing heavy cover.

In order to fish a worm effectively in heavy cover, you have to rig it properly. A number of very sharp plastic worm hooks are on the market. It's worthwhile to experiment with hooks that also rotate, have a raised shank, or have a special bend for greater penetration. No matter what you choose, the hook must be well embedded in the body of the worm to keep the point from becoming snagged. Push the point deep into and almost out of the body of the worm so the soft plastic will offer little resistance and the sharp point will pass through it and into the fish quickly when you set the hook.

Worm fishermen should pay closer attention to hook size. Many use a hook that is exceptionally large, such as 4/0 and 5/0 sizes. Bass may have big mouths, but you don't need big hooks to catch them. Smaller hooks have the added benefit of balancing well with the worm and the weight to produce a better action and make the lure feel more natural to a striking fish. This natural feel is important, because it

Needlepoint Plastic Worms

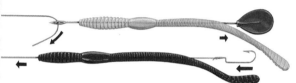

Nothing is more frustrating than missing bass that are short-striking plastic worms. You sense the familiar "tap-tap," respond with a timely hook-set, and hear the swish of your rod slicing the air without resistance. It's like taking a hard cut at a fast ball and never making contact—sort of turns you inside out.

An effective but little-used method for overcoming this dilemma is to thread the line through the center of the worm before tying on the hook. This lets you place a hook farther back in the worm while retaining the lure's natural appearance. When a finicky bass nips at a modified worm, it's not likely to depart without a struggle.

An excellent device for skewering plastic worms is the Rig'R Probe from Tonka Lures in Chanhassen, Minnesota. This tool is essentially a 5-inch needle that has an eyelet near its point. A plastic paddle-shaped handle on the opposite end gives anglers a sure grip when rigging.

Most rigging procedures start by pushing the point of the needle into the worm's tail at the desired hook location. The needle is carefully worked up through the worm and out of its head until only the eye of the needle is exposed on the opposite end.

Thread the needle with the monofilament extending from your rod tip, and string the line through the worm by slowly extracting the needle. Tie on a hook that is appropriate for the thinner, tail end of the worm, usually No. 1 or smaller. Then grasp the line in front of the worm and gently pull it until the shank of the hook is drawn into the bait.

The hook's point may be left exposed when you're fishing in open areas with few snags. If you'll be working the worm through cover, however, bury the barb in the plastic, Texas-style.

When fishing a tail-rigged worm with a slip sinker, peg the weight at the head of the worm by jamming a toothpick into the line hole, and snip off the excess. This prevents the sinker from sliding down, compressing and disfiguring the worm.

An alternative rigging is to thread the line about halfway down the lure, a ploy that works especially well with floating worms. The lure's thicker midsection allows the use of a larger hook.

Another option is a double-hook setup. After implanting a tail-rigged hook, snip off the line about 8 inches in front of the worm. Tie the protruding line to the eye of a plain jig head or a regular worm hook. You'll have to jam the worm down toward the tail hook while doing this, to achieve the proper spacing. Then knot your rod's line to the jig head or hook, and rig it as you normally would.

Needlepoint riggings also work well with other soft-plastic lures, such as jerkbaits, fat grubs, and lizards. They'll prevent you from striking out when bass are biting short.— *Mark Hicks* may cause a bass to hold the worm for just the extra moment you'll need to set the hook.

Weights, especially free-sliding slip sinkers, often cause snagging because they wedge into cracks or crevices or drop over objects while the worm remains behind. Many bass anglers feel that a free-sliding sinker produces the most fish, but when it also causes problems, peg the cavity of the sinker with the tip of a toothpick, fixing it to the fishing line just ahead of the worm. Another option is to use a cone-shaped sinker with a wire fastener. The wire, attached to the bottom of the sinker, works like a corkscrew and is twisted into the center of the head of the worm, keeping the worm and sinker together.

It's important to use the lightest sinker that you can and still be able to feel the bottom and work the worm through heavy cover. A light sinker helps a worm move naturally and enticingly when retrieved. Heavy sinkers deaden worm action but are valuable when you're flipping in heavy cover. Here, you want the worm to drop fast into a particular spot, then be pulled out and flipped to another. Flipping with worms in heavy cover is often overlooked, but it can be better than flipping with jigs, which hang up more readily.

The most common way to fish plastic worms is simply to cast and retrieve them along the bottom. You'll want the worms to hop, crawl, or slither forward slowly in a natural, unalarming manner, perhaps imitating a slow-moving creature or an injured and vulnerable one.

To accomplish this, simply nudge the worm along by raising the rod gently and lowering it quickly, retrieving slack line as you do. It's also helpful to try to make a worm pulse or quiver in place when it's resting on the bottom; you can do this by gently shaking the rod.

There are times when you want to fish a worm over cover instead of through it. This is especially true with submerged vegetation. Soft jerkbait-style worms are excellent here; to retrieve these, jerk the rod tip, reel up slack, and pause before doing it again. Hold the rod at more of a perpendicular angle. You can also use a weightless worm rig tied to a leader, then fastened to a barrel swivel, and retrieved in a constant slow-swimming motion.

When you're fishing in thick cover with plastic worms, use heavy tackle—line in the 10- and 12-pound class and rods capable of horsing big bass out of tough spots. Because of its role in working the worm, detecting strikes, and setting the hook, the rod is the most important part of the rig. Most heavy-cover plastic worm fishing is done with bait-casting tackle, and the better rods have a fast-tapered, slightly limber tip to aid casting, with a strong midsection and butt for setting the hook.

Getting the hook through the plastic worm and into the bass doesn't require any special technique. As soon as you detect a strike, lower the rod tip, reel up slack, and set the hook, all in a wink of time.

After you've unhooked the bass, you'll have to bury the worm in the hook again. If the worm is torn up, which is often the case, use a new one. After all, they're cheap, and there's a few million—or is it billion?—around.

Snakes and Lizards

We can only suppose what plastic worms are meant to imitate, but leeches and snakes are a good guess. Some soft plastics are designed to represent water snakes in head and body shape, and are meant to be fished weightless on the surface. Since a snake in the water is usually on the go, head on the surface, tail propelling it forward, plastic snakes must have a good action body, and they must be retrieved slowly and steadily. When you're sure the fish has taken the lure, strike.

Soft plastic lizards—actually salamander imitations complete with oval head and four short legs—are less commonly used than plastic worms but can be fished in the same manner, both with and without weights. I've had poor success with these soft plastics, but some anglers find them effective in the spring, especially during the spawning period.—*K.S.*

Special Situations

Now it's time to put it all together. You now know the nature of the bass, you know the basic patterns of movement, and you know the best lures and how to use them. This last section deals with several problems that bass fishermen routinely encounter. Problems such as standing timber, muddy water, thick weeds, and dropping water levels. Each presents a unique challenge, and each requires a unique solution. To make matters even more difficult, you may encounter two or more problems at once. How intelligently you face the problem determines whether you get fish or come away empty-handed.

Is there a big secret? You bet. Most times, all it takes is a small adjustment to turn abject failure into rousing success. What separates the *haves* from the *have-nots* is knowing which adjustment to make and when to make it. And that's what you'll learn in the following pages.

Finally, you'll also learn that bass fishing is a lifelong adventure in learning. The smart angler never stops his quest for knowledge. And that is the ultimate compliment for America's Fish.

SINCE 1895

FIELD & STREAM

THE SOUL OF THE AMERICAN OUTDOORS

IN THIS AGE OF MAN-MADE IMPOUNDMENTS, BIG
BOATS, AND MODERN GADGETS, SMALL NATURAL
LAKES ARE OFTEN OVERLOOKED—WHICH IS PRECISELY
WHY YOU SHOULD SEEK THEM OUT.

By Byron W. Dalrymple

Bass, NATURALLY

ASK ANY MODERN BASS enthusiast below age fifty to define a lake, and he'd probably say it's a large body of water behind a dam. Recently, I read about a new, hot bass lake described as "excellent, but rather small—only 11,000-surface acres."

I remember my younger years when I fished Otter, Powderhorn, Heart's, and Birch Lakes, and all had great bass fishing. For 50 cents I'd rent a leaky wooden rowboat complete with anchor—a frayed rope tied to a rock—and a tomato can for bailing. Nobody used a motor on those little lakes. Some days I might see one or two other boats; most days, there were none.

The drastic changes in bass fishing began with projects such as those engineered by the Tennessee Valley Authority. Huge impoundments multiplied and so did the bass, followed by big bass boats, powerful motors, and all the gadgets that go with the sport today. For years I've fished one Texas lake that's 50 miles long, another consisting of 186,000 acres, and many smaller impoundments of only 20,000 to 30,000 acres. I talk to anglers who are familiar with Table Rock in Missouri, Powell in Arizona/Utah, Dale Hollow in Tennessee, Kerr in Virginia, Lewis Smith in Alabama, and a host of other impoundments that are the scene of modern bass fishing.

And then there are lakes such as Raccoon, which lies deep in a Michigan State Forest. To get there, I used to drive a sand trail, getting stuck regularly. My cartop boat was easy to handle alone, and I'd fish motorless, drifting or rowing. The lake wasn't larger than 100 acres, and the fishing was so good that a rank amateur could fill a stringer. I'd fish with bugs mostly; that way I could release them easier. The day I remember most vividly on Raccoon was when I popped my bug beside some cattails, and a bass sucked it in. The fish churned water wildly and streaked off, taking most of my line.

When I finally reeled it in, I found that it weighed 9 pounds—the largest bass I had ever caught in the North. And there is something else I remember about Raccoon: During the years I fished it, I never saw another angler.

Small, natural lakes, which in this impoundment age are virtually forgotten, still offer excellent fishing and enjoyable surroundings. Younger bass anglers may not realize it, but these lakes are where U.S. bass fishing began. Back when the Bass Oreno plug, the Dardevle spoon, and the Hawaiian Wiggler were first cast along shorelines, lakes of 50 to 500 acres were where the action was. A "big" lake consisted of maybe 1,000 acres.

Granted, the hundreds of vast reservoirs built in the last fifty years are the reason for today's tremendous bass fishing popularity. But many have become over-regimented, noisy, and expensive, and they are often crowded.

For the impoundment-weary angler, the small, virtually forgotten, yet surprisingly productive natural lakes offer the simple pleasures of yesterday's bass fishing.

You can find modest-size natural bass lakes in every state, but you seldom hear anything about them. Practically everything written nowadays about bass fishing concerns impoundments and the techniques and equipment used on them. The small, natural lakes differ immensely. Big boats and motors don't fit. All you need is a small skiff, a flatbottom lightweight, or even a canoe. Float tubes will also do the job.

⊷ ⊱⊰ ⊶

MODERN GADGETS—DEPTH finders and such—are more a nuisance than a help. I recall numerous lakes where I've looked for the best bass hangouts just by squinting at shorelines. Most natural lakes that offer good largemouth fishing aren't very deep, usually 20 feet at most. Smallmouth lakes are usually deeper. The surrounding country will also tell you a lot. Where a steep hill borders the lake, the dropoff will be the same. A flat shoreline with reeds will be shallow, and probably sandy. A marshy shoreline with lily pads will have a soft, fertile bottom. Look for smallmouths near rocks or rubble.

An intriguing aspect of fishing natural lakes is that they are highly varied in character. One summer during a trip to Canada, I stopped for a week of fishing in the glacial lakes region of eastern South Dakota. Here, you'll find scores of clear, shallow lakes with excellent angling, and interesting names like Enemy Swim and Blue Dog. I fished a dozen of them, and all provided good bass action. I seldom saw more than one or two small boats. In Georgia one fall, a friend who had wearied of what he called "the dammed lakes" took me to several cypress sloughs and miniature lakes. They used to be fished a lot when he was a kid, but the lure of the big man-made lakes had left them almost deserted, and the bass fishing was truly sensational.

There are scores of oxbow lakes scoured by flooding along big rivers, especially the Mississippi. The Great Lakes Region and the Northeast also offer a number of small naturals that are lightly fished. One summer, near Lake Superior, I camped and fished from shore a lake of about 50 acres, which was full of smallmouths. I asked another fishing camper if he'd tried it. He looked at me as if I was addled. He had a large boat on the big lake, but hadn't caught much.

One of my most interesting experiences on small naturals occurred in Florida, which has few impoundments but does have numerous large lakes teeming with fishermen. I was producing a TV film for a lure manufacturer and we wanted to dodge crowds and the curious, who can ruin filming expeditions. We were told about two tiny naturals deep in a pine forest. One was no larger than 300 yards across, with maiden cane growing near shore. We used a couple of skiffs, filmed for a week, never saw another angler, and caught bass galore. On my wall is a fish from that small lake weighing 12 pounds 6 ounces.

For years one of my greatest bassing pleasures has been shoreline wading in diminutive naturals. Many are hidden in State and National Forests, far from cities. A surprising number in the Great Lakes area and the Midwest are on farms, where you should ask for permission to fish; it's often granted, but sometimes a modest fee is charged. One summer in Montana, irked at balky trout, I tracked down a small forest lake loaded with largemouths. In that trout-famed region, bass were not popular. I fished along stands of reeds, using streamers from my trout fly box. The bass practically fought over them.

For wading in warm lakes, sneakers and old pants will do. In others, you need chest-high waders. Also, you must learn which aquatic plants grow from hard or soft bottoms. Don't take chances in mucky places or you may sink too deep. Stay with sand, gravel, and rocks. The soil along shore invariably will clue you in to what's underwater.

The wader can't carry the voluminous tackle boxes that impoundment anglers are used to. I learned to use small floater-diver plugs, carrying only three or four in a pocket box, plus several spinners and spoons. Bass strike small plugs and medium-size hard lures as eagerly as big ones. Impoundment anglers rarely realize this because they seldom use smaller sizes.

Waders can have a lot of fun fly fishing. There's plenty of backcast room, and fishing flies is not only pleasant, but exceedingly productive. A hot tip I can pass along from much experience is to forget popping bugs for surface fishing. Instead, use medium-size deer-hair lures, because you'll be close to your quarry and need stealth. Deer-hair bugs drop quietly and can be sneaked among pads or reeds, leaving a teasing wake. For sinking flies, be unorthodox. The following trout patterns are deadly: Woolly Worms, Muddlers, and any of the large nymphs.

Mentioning nymphs brings to mind a memorable experience. One year I arranged a guided bass fishing tour of reservoirs in Oklahoma, Kansas, and Nebraska. At every reservoir, the wind blew and rough boating pounded my backside unmercifully. When the wind died down, water skiers and roaring jet skis appeared all over the lake. I'd intended to finish the tour in the Dakotas, but then I remembered Cherry County in the treeless Nebraska range country. Dozens of miniature naturals—the Sandhills Lakes—are located there.

I had a cartop boat with two-piece aluminum oars. Late the next afternoon I slid it into a remote little lake, my fly rod strung with a No. 6 Montana nymph. The action was slow, but the surroundings were wonderful. After I caught three bass, I quit. I'd packed rudimentary camping gear and a grub box. I cooked the fish, feeling sorry for bass addicts born too late to know the simpler pleasures of where it all started. Then I reflected: They could still discover them, for the fishing is as good as ever. I sat a while, enjoying the vast silence. Well, it wasn't completely silent. At dusk, a persistent whippoorwill cranked up.

By Joe Doggett

Bumping the STUMPS

DON'T BE TURNED OFF BY FLOODED FORESTS. LARGEMOUTHS LOVE SUNKEN LOGS, AND IF YOU APPROACH THEM CORRECTLY, YOU WILL TOO.

I WAS STUMPED—NOT an altogether disadvantageous condition on an East Texas bass lake.

Tangles of flooded timber— "stumps"— sprawled across the Lake Livingston cove. I eyed the bounty of limbs and logs and wiggled the light spinning rod. Each gnarly cluster bristled with promise. "Jeez," I said. "Where do I chunk?"

My friend, Jack Segall, shrugged. "Just use your instincts. But you ought to be throwing a heavy casting rod. Bumping the stumps is no place for a wet-noodle rig."

Just ahead, an exceptional logjam fanned across the surface. Dark shadows filtered into the rich green. I dropped a 7-inch weighted black worm into the tangle, and the coils of descending line promptly rushed tight. I reared back. The limber rod doubled. The 8-pound monofilament sawed against a burst of power, and the upwelling boil of the digging sow was punctuated by abrupt slack. A "piggy tail" of broken line trailed across the surface.

Segall shook his head. "Well, that's what you get for bringing a knife to a gun fight." He held out a casting rig spooled with 20-pound line. "Here, get serious and use the right stuff."

That long-ago incident was a reminder that fishing the timber is a specialized drill. Most dammed lakes are filled with trees—the natural vegetation that was inundated as the impoundment filled. These flooded woods may frustrate regattas and runabouts, but they are strong allies to serious anglers.

For one thing, bass favor this cover. As the old East Texas expression goes, lunkers and logs are as inseparable as cigar smoke and poker chips. Flooded timber offers security and shade, and provides good camouflage for ambush-oriented bass waiting to lunge after passing forage.

Second, the casting targets are well defined. A log or a stump offers a tight strike

Dammed lakes are often filled with trees that scare away water skiers and swimmers, but attract big bass. To take them, you'll need to cast close, navigate with caution, and use appropriate heavy tackle.

zone (although in some cases, depth must be considered). If a bass is home, the presentation will be pointblank. Work your spot, then move to the next target. This efficient pattern evokes confidence.

Third, this is fishing-only water. The standing timber discourages interference from the dancing bears, jugglers, and clowns of assorted weekend circuses. Good luck water skiing or jet skiing or wind surfing through a stump field. Even other fishing boats must move slowly and cautiously through your fishing area. This forced courtesy is no small trump on crowded public water.

Finally, big-fish potential soars. Heavy old sows are remarkably fond of heavy logs and limbs. You can take a Paul Bunyan attitude into the timber, and fish with the conviction that a career bass might be within reach.

Years ago, a friend of mine, Forrest West,

was fishing a timbered river on Texas' Lake Sam Rayburn. His nine-year-old son, Jimmy, was sharing the boat. Jimmy, with the magic of a Lotto winner, dabbled a spinnerbait into a boatside logjam. A big bass clamped down. Unaided, the young angler fought the fish through logs, around the bow, and into the waiting net.

Jimmy's bass weighed 9 pounds 11 ounces. As his father stared at the gleaming hulk, Jimmy again dropped the spinnerbait into the logs and stuck another bass. This one scaled 10 pounds 3 ounces.

Jimmy, deciding that bass fishing was pretty easy, made ready for another try. West grabbed his boy by the nape of his neck, depositing him in the stern. "Son, stand aside! Let me show you how it's done."

West fed the marvelous logs a 9-inch black worm. A mauling strike wrenched the rod and he struggled back and forth, up and down, as the fish churned mud clouds around the shuddering limbs. With a final pump and heave, the excited angler saw his catch—a 15-pound blue catfish.

"Thanks, Dad," said Jimmy. "Now you've wrecked my hole."

Big fish, even those without whiskers, haunt the timber. The problem, unless you happen to be fishing with Jimmy West, is finding them. A maze of flooded timber can be confounding. Too many targets are available.

The key is to select the most promising bass holding sites. For example, a logjam associated with aquatic weeds rates higher than a similar nearby structure in open water. A leaning trunk or blowdown provides more cover and shade than a vertical tree. On the subject of shade, remember that during periods of high sun, bass usually hang on the shadowed side of a stump or log.

The influence of shade may not be as critical in deep or murky water, but it is always worth considering. Bass, being muggers by nature, dislike the spotlight.

The astute "woodsman" can scan a cove and use the flooded timber to help map the bottom. A meandering line of cypress or willows, trees that favor moist soil, may mark an old creek channel inundated by the reservoir. A rough oval suggests the banks of an old farm pond.

Conversely, a cluster of pines may point to a ridge or hump. Pines prefer sandy soil, as do spawning bass and bluegills. None of this is absolute, but taking a moment to study the distribution and type of timber in an area might provide usable information for the keen angler.

Bass are "edge" creatures. They tend to hang along the breaks of shadowed canopies. Any defined tree line is worth a few casts—especially if the bottom contour abruptly changes. The outside edges and road beds are obvious and usually hard hit; therefore, the ability to locate a narrow channel winding inside the thick timber (remember those willows?) can be a big trump on a public reservoir.

Timbered coves and shorelines are boldly evident, so they may draw a disproportionate amount of weekend and vacation fishing traffic The inexperienced boater must understand that unusual hazards exist.

Timber is "hard" cover. It doesn't give. This point will be driven home to you when, at high speed, you center-punch a stump. Use caution when running outside marked lanes or when approaching any shallow and stump-riddled water. And keep in mind that the water level on a dammed reservoir can fluctuate dramatically, often with little warning. Fluctuations of more than a foot or so can drastically alter the composition of a mine field of stumps and logs. The safe course through the old '"Alligator Slough" you charted a month ago may now be bogus. Ask for updates at the marinas, and respect the advice of the regulars.

The standing timber in an older reservoir is, for the most part, dead and brittle. The battering of a high wind can break limbs, or even trunks. Do not get caught in a cove of towering skeletons in a low-pressure situation and, regardless of wind velocity, abandon the water if thunder threatens. Surely some frazzled golfer has warned you about trees and lightning.

Even running the battery-powered troll motor demands respect. Should you plow into a submerged log, be cautious when backing off. Most units are not well-protected when running in reverse. If the whirring blade jams another log, the impact may shear the prop, a fact that the paddling blisters on my hands will attest to.

Use caution when attempting to dislodge a boat from a submerged log or stump. Several years ago, I was guiding a lady friend on a private pond near Houston. The water was riddled with timber and known to hold jumbo bass. I had just bagged a 6-pounder and was feeling pretty cocky when I hung the skiff out to dry on a big stump.

"Sit down and hold on," I instructed my partner. "I'll rock us free."

I hopped to the bow, swayed right and left, and goosed the troll motor as the hull started to slide. Instantly, I was underwater. I went over so fast, my eyes were still open; I recall peering through a misty blur of bubbles and seeing a costly pair of Vuarnet sunglasses settle past.

Bloody hell, I thought. *Surely I haven't fallen over. Only potlickers fall out of boats.*

My friend, acting quickly, vaulted to the bow and cut the troll motor. Blowing and heaving, sputtering and gagging, festooned in coontail moss, I rolled into the skiff. My friend stared down and attempted a show of grave concern that spilled into a huge laugh.

"Where's your fishing rod?" she asked.

The rig—a new high-tech graphite casting rod fitted with a state-of-the-art magnetic casting reel—was last sighted at 10 yards from the skiff, tilted at about 11 o'clock, slanting down. I peered uncertainly at the gloomy, snag-filled depths. Like many ponds in southeast Texas, our host water harbored alligators of all sizes, which were no doubt living in tandem with wriggling leeches. Jurassic Pond.

"Oh, that old rig was a piece of junk," I said.

"You're just afraid to go get it," she answered.

Five minutes of desperate duck-diving and face-saving later, I retrieved the errant tackle. Of course, the effort routed all bass from the area.

Bass living amid heavy timber are easy to approach, assuming you stay in the boat. The fish are aware of the security provided by massive logs and, except under extreme high-visibility or shallow circumstances, can be pressed to tight quarters. Close casting is the high-percentage choice. Cast long, and you forfeit accuracy and authority.

Work closely and try to go inside. Only meek amateurs are satisfied with hitting the near edge. Chunk beyond a vertical tree, cutting the shadowed corner, and rake the side or cross the top of a submerged log. Use a flip or pitch to drop a weighted, snagless offering inside a tangle of limbs. And don't be afraid to rattle the cage.

Banging or bumping the lure into the timber, either on the delivery or during the retrieve, helps telegraph opportunity to lurking bass. Remember, the unalerted fish underneath the cover feels secure, and the churning vibrations of wounded or disoriented prey trigger its killer instinct.

Effective tools for bumping the stumps are safety-pin spinnerbaits and long-lipped crankbaits. These lures feature snagless designs that allow aggressive contact with hard cover. Flutter or "slow roll" the spinner over the limbs, and grind and root the crankbait against the logs and trunks, even into the bottom. When bass are less aggressive, try coaxing a slow-moving bait such as a lead-head jig or a snagless plastic worm or lizard through the clutter. Fish suspended on deeper timber can be vertically jigged with heavy spoons. Regardless of lure selection, employ the heaviest "string" that you can get away with under the circumstances. Timber rustlers in most murky-green lakes employ 15- to 25-pound-test line.

When the lure stops, strike hard and fast. This is no time for a tentative response. Rear back with gusto and hope you hang a 5-pound black bass, rather than a 500-pound brown log. If, indeed, the counterpunch moves, keep lifting and cranking, trying to uproot the startled fish before it can dive and wrap.

Remember that the timber is no place for finesse. Hooking a fine bass is a hollow victory, and an insult to conservation, if you break off with inadequate tackle. Consider the size of the fish that haunt these holes, and arm yourself with appropriate gear. You want to get stumped—not skunked.

By Philip Bourjaily

FARM POND BASS

THE LARGEMOUTH
BASS IS A CELEBRATED
TRANSPLANT THAT
THRIVES IN
SMALL PONDS.

STAN RETRIEVES HIS lure, cranking the reel handle with gnarled fingers. It's said of baseball catchers that shaking their hands feels like squeezing a bag full of peanuts, but foul tips can't begin to smash fingers the way wagon hitches and power takeoffs can. Compared to old farmers like Stan, catchers have the hands of concert pianists.

"You hear those city people say we don't have any nature left," he says, making a long cast toward shore. "They should come out and see this."

From my seat in the bow I see a landscape completely remade by the hand of man on the throttle of a bulldozer. Beyond the shoreline, terraced rows of corn surround us on all sides, nearly head-high under the July sun. Waves of heat mirage shimmer above the tassels. In the distance, a thin line of trees marks the course of the straightened creek.

We're fishing a small farm pond, formed by three earthen walls pushed up around a wet spot at the bottom of a hill. The water is warm and murky, much too much so for any trout, walleye, or smallmouth ever to call it home. Fortunately for us, largemouth bass think pond water's just fine; Stan's dinner is finning stoically on his stringer, and we've caught and released any number of smaller fish.

Largemouths don't merely survive in the hundreds of thousands of farm ponds into which they've been introduced across the country—they prosper. Given enough bluegills for roughage, a farm pond bass can grow to state-record size, such as the 13-pound 2-ounce fish

from Ohio or the 11-pound 12-ouncer from a Kansas "tank." Unlike such accomplished survivors as the carp or the English sparrow, the farm pond largemouth is as sporty as it is adaptable. That trait elevates the fish to the level of the ringneck pheasant, another celebrated transplant (albeit from much farther away) which thrives in grainfields that haven't seen a prairie chicken in decades.

From a sportsman's point of view, the two are not without their similarities. Overalls and 870s are proper attire for pheasants anywhere worth hunting them, and those same overalls, plus a spinning rod and a small rowboat, are all the gear you need for pond bassing. A cock pheasant or a decent pond bass makes a meal by itself, which still matters to people no more than two generations removed from the farm.

We call one a rooster, the other a hog, correctly implying you needn't travel much farther than your uncle's place to find either one. Pheasants and bass both lurk invisible, under heavy cover, but neither is much for subtlety when it's time to commit, whether flushing raucously from a cornfield or blasting through the algae to engulf a frog.

Last fall, the distinction between the two blurred over completely for me when I shot a rooster on a raw November morning, dropping him into the middle of a farm pond. The stiff wind was supposed to push him to shore where my nonswimming dog and I waited. Instead, the bird hung up on a snag where, on a warmer day, I'd once tossed plugs at a bass. That recollection gave me an idea. I went down to the farmhouse, came back with a borrowed spinning rod and a Flatfish, and snared the pheasant and reeled him in.

As I unhooked the dripping rooster, the scene suddenly made a certain, skewed sense: a pheasant probably would take a lure like a Flatfish, or perhaps a noisy, bright-yellow plug imitating an escaping kernel of corn. Not, at any rate, a size 18 Adams. And a bass might cackle if it vocalized at all. Nothing less than a load of high-brass 5s would knock a largemouth down consistently.

We will consider the correct choke and barrel length for bass another time and return to the subject of catching them on rod and reel. Farm pond bass fishing is rarely a matter of covering water, prospecting for fish. In fact, since many farm ponds aren't all that much bigger than Olympic pools, you're presenting your lures to a captive audience. One pond I fish frequently is about 1 acre in size, basically just a clay bowl full of water, and the farmer keeps the grass on the banks shorter than most suburban lawns. The bottom of his pond is as neat as the ground around it. In addition to bass, he's stocked white amur, a kind of large grass-eating carp from Asia, which trim the algae and aquatic plants the way a flock of sheep mows a pasture. In a pond as featureless as this one, the bass are everywhere and nowhere in particular. You just walk around the edge, casting, figuring your lure must never be far from a fish.

Most farm ponds offer a little more in the way of structure to shelter the fish and focus the fisherman—a point or two, a few snags, maybe a stand of cattails. If the farmer is a serious fisherman, he may have even dumped some brush and old Christmas trees into the water, weighing them down with cinder blocks. The most important cover for pond bass, however, are weeds and algae.

By late June, the plants have grown so thick that shore fishing most ponds becomes nearly impossible—and no fun at all. Any fish you hook quickly entangles itself in so many pounds of muskgrass that it feels more like a snagged truck tire. Better then to fish from a float tube, a fiberglass canoe, or one of those miniature plastic bass boats that fit in the back of a van. From a boat in the middle of the pond,

you can cast to the edge of the weedbeds and let an unweighted worm flutter slowly down past the bass hanging suspended in the nooks and crannies among the weeds. Often, bass will dart out and grab your lure the instant it touches water, buttonhooking immediately for the safety of the weeds. I always try to cast perpendicular to the weedline, so I can more easily snub a hooked fish out into open water and away from the greenery.

Although you'll concentrate along the shoreline, don't neglect the middle of the pond. There may not be any apparent structure, but bass are out cruising the open water, like small-town teenagers with nothing to do. These idlers can usually be convinced to strike a spinner or Twister Tail. Often, too, bass will crowd around a motionless surface lure, eyeing it balefully until one decides to give it a whack.

Early in the year, up until spawning time, the water will be open enough for you to stalk the banks, looking for bass on the nests. A plastic worm plopped into their nests, or a large Rapala dragged past their noses will sometimes irritate them into striking. Even without polarized glasses, it's easy to spot spawning bass in the shallows. Crowds of bluegills and smaller bass look on, loitering quietly until one small fish strays across an invisible boundary and the bass scatters the whole group with a threatening rush. Before the ripples have faded, all the fish are back where they were, motionless again.

My biggest pond bass was a spawning female, caught on a May afternoon when I was ten years old. The huge, aloof fish showed no interest whatsoever in my jointed minnow, no matter how many times I retrieved it across her path. Finally, one cast, no different from any of its predecessors, provoked a mild strike. Tiring of the annoyance, the bass picked up the lure to move it out of the nest, and I set the hook. Since the fish hit all of 3 feet from the rod tip, it was not so much a matter of playing it as simply allowing the bass to beach herself, after which I let her go. Even at that age I knew spawners should be returned to the water, both the trophy females and the smaller males who guard the eggs.

Bass like those are very much the big fish in small ponds you hear about. Although they're the masters of their 3-acre domains, they can be intimidated by the sight of a big, garish spinnerbait and pork rind. The typical bassing rig—bait-casting rod, heavy line, and big lures—doesn't fare as well on these small ponds. Switch to light or even ultralight spinning rods, lighter lines, and smaller lures. That said, it must be admitted that pond bass lack the jaded sophistication of impoundment fish which see dozens of different metal-flake hulls motoring by every weekend. The pond fish are often underfished, and they seem always to be hungry—so much so that sometimes I'm guilty of taking them for granted. If an especially cranky mood strikes, I'll dismiss man-made ponds and their stocked bass populations among the cornfields as little better than those roadside "fishing" attractions where you can catch all the half-bright trout you want on doughballs for so much per pound.

When I start thinking those thoughts, it's time to see my familiar waters through someone else's eyes again, and I invite someone fishing. Last summer I took a widely traveled angler out after work late one afternoon. Through some adroit four-wheeling he maneuvered his boat and trailer to a secluded pond in a wood-lot and backed it in. As we pushed the boat into the water, a great blue heron flushed ponderously into the sky, neck held in a tight S, long legs trailing behind, looking to me, as these birds always do, like some last, lonely pterodactyl. We heard the slap of a beaver's tail, and doves cooed their melancholy note.

The boat was a 16-foot V-bottom, far bigger than needed for a farm pond, but so stable we could both walk around in it as if we were fishing from a small island. With the trolling motor pulling us along silently, parallel to the shore, we worked the weeds by the dam first, catching several smaller fish and a couple of nice ones. During lulls between strikes the conversation turned to fishing trips—to Saskatchewan, Minnesota, Lake Oahe, and the Roaring Fork in Colorado—my guest having been many places and having far more stories to tell than I.

"You know," I finally said apologetically, "these days, I don't get to travel much. I have to do all my fishing right here."

The swallows had come out, skimming low over the water in graceful curves. My guest said earnestly, "If I had a pond like this, I wouldn't fish anywhere else."

Behind us, out in the cornfields, we heard a rooster pheasant crow.

By Joe Doggett

CROWD CONTROL

INTREPID BASSERS WHO PLACE FISHING FOREMOST FIND WAYS TO KEEP THE MOB AT A DISTANCE. BUT NOT EVERYONE WANTS TO BE ALONE…

THE WIND IS LIGHT, the air is mild, the weekend is long, and I might be your biggest setback to catching bass. Well, perhaps not me, specifically, but the "other guy" who competes with you for the available hot spots on chosen water.

The crowded launch ramp is a common denominator on most public lakes and reservoirs, and the competition from other anglers is a factor that should be considered as you measure the potential of a trip. Naturally, the crowd factor rears its ugly head (make that heads) under the most positive circumstances—those days and places that beg for a hungry cast.

A nearby public lake with a recent history of big catches is certain to draw a "cast of thousands." That's just a fact. Sunny weekends further curdle the mix by attracting hordes of recreational boaters. When the snarling wakes of jet skis and speed boats collide with courtesy and common sense, and everything but a bearded lady and a dancing bear is thrashing the water, well, that's a tough draw.

The obvious solution is to dodge the big weekends and target the relatively uncrowded midweek. Call in sick or use a vacation day, or cut out of work early to take advantage of the lengthening daylight.

Unfortunately, this strategy works better in theory than it does in practice. Many of us do not have the schedule flexibility that would allow us to concentrate on the "ice cream" days, and so we are forced by necessity to cross wakes with the weekend pack.

You could forfeit the hot lake and fish elsewhere, but that's like admitting you can't run with

the A-Team. You don't want to downgrade to Perch Lake or Carp Lake—but I'm in line before you, and a dozen boats are looming ahead of me, and twenty more rigs are trailering up the road behind you. Fortunately, there are ways to minimize the impact of the other guy.

PUT YOUR BEST foot forward. In short, try wade fishing. Run your boat to a tangled stretch of shorelines, then hop over the side and go in after 'em. I am convinced that this simple technique remains one of the most overlooked trumps in bass fishing. Any lake, large or small, offers choice shorelines and shallows that are suitable for a soggy soft shuffle, and many of these areas, which are often rimmed by timber and weed mats, go virtually untapped by boat traffic. The outside edges get whipped by the ongoing parade while the inside edges and pot-holes go begging.

Some of these areas may not look like much from the outside, but once you ease past

the perimeter, the water may open into a mean-dering slough or creek channel. More fishable water than a glance from the open lake suggests is almost always available "back in there." These tight backwaters can be difficult to cover from a boat. The brush and weeds are too thick and the hull is too noisy, which makes the whole drill an exercise in frustration. Explosive blooms of aquatic vegetation promise to make the situation even worse during the long, hot days of summer.

But the old two-step is a great way to ambush bass that are holding amid shallow tangles. By wading quietly, you can position yourself close for accurate and repeated casts to a specific target. You can also plant yourself against the wind without drifting or back-pedaling, and you can maintain a low profile. These are degrees of stealth that the banging, bumping boater cannot match.

Trading in your bass boat for a pair of wading booties does restrict the size of your fishing area, but don't be put off by a lack of mobility. A big lake does not demand a full tank of gas—a fact that many fast-lane bass boaters fail to accept. One-hundred yards of shoreline or creek channel is enough territory to provide a great morning or afternoon session for the determined and methodical wader. If you do your homework and select a stretch of quality water, you can step inside the crowds and reach unhassled bass.

TRY MOONLIGHTING. Most serious anglers know the wisdom of night moves, but surprisingly few actually practice nocturnal fishing. If you are chunking under the stars, rather than under the sun, you have automatically eliminated most of the boating traffic.

A night session will insure an abundance of serene water on even the most pressure-packed weekends. As a general rule, nights when the moon shines bright are best; bass seem to feed more aggressively under a clear sky, and the visibility is improved.

But regardless of moon phase, becoming "one with the owls" or fishing all night is a bit extreme, and such a power play may not be necessary. Modifying the drill and balancing the night session with an hour or two of prime low-light fishing is a more workable compromise. You can hit the water during the late afternoon and fish through dusk to 10 or 11 P.M. Or you can launch at 3 or 4 A.M. and be sitting on a choice site for the dawn patrol. By utilizing either approach, you'll minimize traffic and be in position to take advantage of daylight for one run across the lake. And by gaining a few hours of sleep, you won't be a wiped-out zombie the next day.

Night fishing does require special considerations. The temperature might be cool, especially if conditions are windy, so pack an extra layer of clothing. Bugs might also present a problem; don't forget to bring a supply of no-nonsense repellent. Keep your running lights in order and your flotation jacket handy and be ready for things that go bump in the night. Like big bass.

GO AGAINST THE grain. Certain areas on a popular lake will draw the heaviest traffic on a given day. This concentration of effort is usually the result of recent fishing reports. Lucky the Guide and Ace the Pro "killed 'em" in Caney Creek, and word for the weekend spreads on the levelwind telegraph.

Leave Caney Creek to the rest of the pack. The anointed water will be flailed to a froth under the crush of boats. Lucky and Ace might have had a great catch, but the odds that the fishing will hold through the big weekend are between Slim and None. And Slim just got a terrible backlash.

Instead of chasing the herd, try to evaluate the circumstances—the "pattern"—that produced the big catch. If the bass came from the edges of the Caney Creek channel, say from 5- or 6-foot water falling into 10- or 12-foot depths, locate a similar pattern in another creek. Ideally, the new water will offer similar cover, clarity, and temperature.

If you cannot find a workable alternative, try ranging out and fishing points. "Getting to the point" is an excellent way to locate bass on big water. Points of land that extend into a lake serve as ambush areas for bass and provide a wide range of depth within close reach. These are easy to locate and easy to fish, and those with favorable cover—weeds or stickups or rocks—are bass magnets. It doesn't take much of a point to hold fish; a mere thumb near the bend of a channel might make your day. Also, the small and inconspicuous points are less likely to be trampled by the crowds.

Go hunting, hopping from one likely spot to the next. The idea is to cover select areas quickly, and a good way to do this is by rapid-fire casting with crankbaits or spinnerbaits. These lures are relatively snagless and they can run from shallow to deep to reach the available potential.

Although you'll never be able to make crowds disappear, you can make them less intrusive. The key is to keep moving against the grain, and find your own fish.

By Mark Hicks

HIGH NOON

CONTRARY TO POPULAR
BELIEF, BASS MAY BITE
BEST UNDER A BLAZING
MIDDAY SUN.

brow? If so, you're not alone. Launching ramps
are busy just before noon as fishermen hastily
load their boats and make tracks for the shade.
What many anglers fail to realize is that bass
also seek shade at midday, a trait that often
makes them easier to locate and catch.

Traditional thinking has it that bass feed
up early and late in the day and retreat to the
depths and stop biting when the sun is high.
The advantages of fishing during the low light
hours are chiseled in stone, but you also should
accept the fact that many bass remain shallow
throughout the day and will readily take a shot
at a well-presented lure.

Scientists tracking largemouths by radio
telemetry have found that bass will stay in
water less than 6 feet deep even when the surface temperature is over 90 degrees, provided
they have adequate cover. I've taken many largemouths less than 3 feet deep under such bath-
water conditions. Successful bass tournament
anglers who must fish the midday hours during
competition frequently make excellent catches
under a high, scorching sun.

WHEN THE SUN BURNS
off the morning mist and
cranks up the heat, does your zeal for
bass fishing evaporate like the sweat from your

You needn't be a scientist or a tournament angler to understand and catch high-noon bass. First bear in mind that bass in low light tend to roam more, relate loosely to cover and swim farther to intercept your lures. The "strike zone" is larger at these times, so you don't have to get your lures as close to the fish to encourage a positive response. Bass may be swimming over submerged weeds, for example, or cruising around underwater stump rows or flooded brush. Retrieving lures over or near these and other forms of cover will readily attract bass that are in an active feeding mode.

When hard sunlight penetrates the surface at midday, however, bass move tighter to cover, and lurk in the shadows. Instead of swimming above submergent weeds, they may drop down into openings in the vegetation and stay near the bottom. Bass will bury under weeds that form a canopy on the surface, such as lily pads and matted milfoil and hydrilla. Here they will also find cooler water. Instead of relating to the edges of brush, fallen trees, and other wood cover, bass hold tight to the darkest shadows. The strike zone grows smaller, so accurate casting and precise lure placement become crucial.

High-noon bass anglers who keep their lures probing the shade have it made with heavier catches. One of my favorite noontime covers is a fallen log or snag on a shallow flat, which is an ideal spot for taking bass with a spinnerbait. Before casting, I'll size up the cover and find the most prominent shadow. The shadow will be directly under the cover when the sun is at its zenith, but before and after this period it will be on one side of the object.

Whenever possible, position the boat so you can cast beyond the cover and retrieve the spinnerbait parallel to it through the entire length of the shadow. The first cast usually does the job, so make it count. Missing the shadow by a only a foot may not pull the bass from its lair, particularly in murky water. Casting to the sunny sides of objects is low-percentage fishing compared with concentrating on the shadows.

The same principles apply to many other bass covers regardless of the lure you're fishing. The object may be a stump, dock, or windfall and your lure a plastic worm, crankbait, or buzzbait. Look for the shadows, fish them relentlessly, and strikes will soon be forthcoming.

Running crankbaits and spinnerbaits over submerged weeds may get fast action in low light, but when the sun gets high and the bass sink into the vegetation, you'll generally coax more strikes with a weedless plastic worm. Go with a large worm that won't get lost in the greenery, such as an 8-incher, and use a slip sinker heavy enough to pull the worm down into the weeds, say 3/16 to 3/8 ounce. Peg the weight by jamming a round toothpick into the line hole on the bottom of the sinker and breaking off the excess. Push the sinker down to the head of the worm and it will stay put, preventing the weight and worm from becoming separated.

Short casts will allow you to work the worm down into the weeds more efficiently and improve your ability to feel strikes. Also concentrate on weed edges, especially points and inside turns.

Matted vegetation requires a shift in tackle from a stiff worm-action rod with 12- to 14-pound line to a long, stout flippin' stick with 17- to 25-pound-test. Match the worm with a heavier bullet weight that will bust through the surface weeds and reach bass in the open water below. That means 1/2 ounce or more depending on the density of the weeds. Thick, isolated clumps near deep water are often the most productive.

You'll also want to wield a flippin' rod when fishing brushy cover at high noon, since bass will back right into the heart of it. A compact lure penetrates brush more easily than a

long worm, and you really don't need a large lure because it won't get lost in brush the way it can in weeds. A 6-inch worm or 4-inch plastic crawfish rigged weedless serves well. Hookguard jigs with rubber skirts and pork or plastic trailers are also good bets, even though many anglers regard them as cool-water lures.

Here again, look for the darkest shadows and flip your offerings through whatever openings are available. The thicker the brush, the more time you should give the bass to locate the lure. You may have to work it up and down several times in one location before finally getting a strike. Many anglers also use flippin' rods for slinging slop baits, such as weedless spoons and surface rats and frogs. Working these lures over lily pads and matted weeds at midday can result in explosive strikes, and the heavy rod is just the thing for extracting a big bass wadded in weeds. You may find untapped bass fishing by employing a push pole and working far back into weed-choked flats and bays where few anglers are willing to go.

Even though the water is clear, the aquatic vegetation provides bass with ample cover to make them feel at ease in the shallows. Stained water is better when it comes to fishing wood cover at high noon, however, because bass in murky water usually don't require as much wood to hold them under bright sunlight as do bass in clear water. A single stickup or a sparse bush may host a substantial bass in dingy water. Since the water clarity is less than 2 feet, bass are less likely to see you and spook before you cast.

Murky water isn't necessarily mud-stained. The milky color is frequently a tip-off to high fertility and plentiful plankton. Shad and other baitfish thrive in such environments, and so do

bass. Some murky bass waters are actually better during midday than at any other time. Many high-noon specialists avoid clear water and key on murky lakes, ponds, or the dingier, upriver creek arms of large impoundments. You'd be wise to do the same if you have any of these options in your area.

One place you'll often find stained water even in clear lakes is on windy banks. When the wind gets up at midday and pushes waves into soft banks, it often creates a mudline that attracts baitfish and bass. On calm, sunny days when boaters abound, the excessive traffic may create mudlines and actually stir up good fishing. This is one of the few times you may be thankful for water skiers.

Should your enthusiasm begin wilting in the heat, keep in mind that some of the largest bass on record were taken at midday. Many knowledgeable anglers are convinced that the high noon hours yield the biggest bass, including Bill O'Connor of Clewiston, Florida, who has been a bass guide for decades. During the winter months O'Connor treats his clients to oversized largemouths on Lake Okeechobee; in the summer he moves his base to Clayton, New York, and guides for largemouths and smallmouths on the Thousand Islands region of the St. Lawrence River. O'Connor's clients have taken thousands of big bass, including hundreds over 10 pounds from Florida waters. Almost all of the trophy specimens have come between the hours of 10 A.M. and 2 P.M.

"If you want to catch big bass consistently," says O'Connor, "you can't be afraid of the heat."

Before venturing out under potentially torrid conditions, take precautions against the sun's harsh rays. Apply sunscreen liberally, wear sunglasses that have 100 percent UV protection, and drink plenty of water throughout the day.

If you can put up with the heat, high-noon bass fishing will produce additional bites, and it may well provide the best action of the day—perhaps even the biggest bass of your life.

By Joe Doggett

Making the
MOST
OF MUD

RATHER THAN RUNNING FROM
OFF-COLOR WATER, USE IT TO
YOUR ADVANTAGE.

MUDDY WATER IS A discouraging element on any bass lake. A flush of coffee-stained currents is a major disruption, and nobody except maybe Juan Valdez of "mountain grown" fame feels entirely at home on brown water.

But experienced anglers know how to make the most of mud. Professional guides, especially, must learn to consistently catch bass from off-color water.

"Muddy water is not always as bad as it looks," says Gene Ballard, a top guide on heavily fished Fayette County Reservoir in southeast Texas. "A lot of good bass can be caught from really dirty shorelines.

"One key is to fish shallow—sometimes in a foot or two of water. The reduced visibility of muddy water provides cover, and bass feel secure moving tight to the banks. Lots of fishermen hit the shorelines, but they are fishing in 4 or 5 feet of water. They don't reach those fish right on the banks."

Lure choice can also determine whether you'll draw strikes in muddy water. Since ambush-oriented bass in poor-visibility conditions rely more on sound than sight for locating prey, a lure that transmits strong vibrations gets the nod.

"It's hard to beat a big spinnerbait," said Ballard. "I prefer the oval Colorado-type blades over the slimmer willow-leaf type for muddy water. The wide face of the Colorado blade creates a deeper, stronger pulse even with a slow retrieve. I'd say use a spinnerbait and blade

that's one size larger than your normal choice when you're looking at a muddy shoreline. Try slow-rolling it over stickups and logs and let it flutter into those weedbed pockets."

Along dropoff edges, Ballard often chunks a deep-diving crankbait. "It's the same deal as the spinnerbait—a bigger plug with a bigger, wider lip that'll really wobble. If it digs down and bumps bottom, so much the better."

Jim Morris, owner of Cypress Creek Marina on Toledo Bend Reservoir, has fished and guided on that sprawling Texas/Louisiana bass factory for seventeen years. He is also no stranger to making the most of mud, especially during late winter and early spring when heavy rains can trigger major runoffs in the lake's tributary creeks. The same areas can be excellent fishing sites, since pre-spawning and spawning bass move shallow in the warming water to feed and fan nests.

"I always like to match the available forage," said Morris. "A good way to do this in muddy water is to check the banks. If the bank is made of clay, chances are that crawfish are the primary forage. Crawfish live in the clay and soft mud, and the 'mud bugs' are a major spring forage for bass—not just in Toledo Bend, but wherever they're found.

sion. Most important, bass lurking nearby can see the image. A quiet lure in a subdued color and realistic profile does absolutely no good if a surly bass 5 feet away cannot sense its approach.

"The bright colors help, but you can get carried away," Morris cautions. "I like to stay within the natural color schemes of prey—I just exaggerate them."

When imitating shad or bluegills, Morris favors white/chartreuse or yellow/chartreuse. When crawfish are the call, he dredges near bottom with orange/black or red/black. "Black is overlooked. Bass in dirty water can see black pretty well, and black is one of the natural colors on some crawfish," says Morris.

Ballard also backs using bright and contrasting colors in murky water. "You can mix things up with a spinnerbait by adding a bright trailer of some sort—a dyed pork rind or a short plastic tail that flutters. That big, upturned single hook on a spinnerbait makes using a trailer ideal. You can even add a stinger hook for short strikes."

Rigged with or without a stinger, the trailer increases the image and action of the safety-pin spinnerbait. It's a trump that more anglers should try. As another consideration, a buoyant trailer of soft plastic or pork slows the sink rate of a spinnerbait.

"Bass in muddy water may have trouble sensing and reacting to a lure," said Ballard. "The lure needs to be moving and fluttering, but the longer you can keep it in the strike zone around a brushpile or logjam, the better the chance that a bass can find it and nail it.

"Spinnerbaits and crankbaits are great because they create a lot of vibration and flash. You can fish shallow water—fast or slow—and they don't get snagged all the time. That's important. The bass are tattooed right to the cover. They'll eat, but when the water's muddy, you've got to get in there and wake 'em up."

"If the banks are sandy, the primary forage is likely to be some sort of finfish such as bream (bluegills and sunfish) or threadfin shad. Either way, the bank can tell you about the forage even if the shallows are too off-color to see much."

Morris, like Ballard, rates the spinnerbait and crankbait as the most effective one-two punch for farming mud.

"Sound is the trigger when bass can't see, and that means a big-bladed spinnerbait or a crankbait that really digs and wobbles. And a crankbait that rattles puts you ahead of the game. I don't think there's any doubt that a rattling-type plug is a plus in dirty water."

Morris supports bold and contrasting color schemes. Turbid water may discourage bass from sight feeding, but the reduced visibility does not eliminate this natural instinct. A largemouth in shallow, warming water is a headhunter, and bright colors can elicit a reflexive strike from a close fish. Mixing the bright colors adds jive to a monotone offering, and materials with metalflake or sparkle spice the draw. Such dazzlers might appear overly dramatic or even outrageous when dangling from a rod tip, but dirty water diffuses the brash colors and creates a believable impres-

By Steve Price

RESULTS, *Not* EXCUSES

EVERY BASS FISHERMAN gets skunked from time to time. Though the actual reasons may vary, the excuses often have a familiar ring: the water was too cold, too hot, too clear, too muddy, or rising or falling too fast.

But if you're really interested in results, not just excuses, you need to learn how to deal with changing water conditions. Since the most drastic of these are rising and falling water levels, sudden temperature changes, and incoming mud, we'll concentrate our efforts here.

INCOMING MUD

MY FIRST ENCOUNTER with fast-rising muddy water occurred years ago on the Tennessee River. Heavy thunderstorms had left Wheeler Lake looking like yesterday's feed lot. My partner Bill Huntley suggested taking along shovels so we could dig holes in the mud to get to the fish. I spent the day plowing shallow coves with a crankbait and came in with one 3-pounder. Huntley raced down the lake where the mud wasn't as bad, worked a small spinnerbait along the edge of some grassbeds, and returned with a livewell full of bass.

"The first thing to remember about muddy water is that it brings bass shallow," Huntley says. "I don't believe it's because they have difficulty breathing, but because the baitfish do, and the bass simply follow them.

"Because of the rain, we also had fast-rising water, which also pushes bass shallow. All I had to do was get ahead of the worst mud, which I did by going down the lake, pulling into a quiet cove, and fishing a weedy, grass-lined bank. The bass were right where they were supposed to be."

Four-time world bass-fishing champion Rick Clunn echoes Huntley's assertion. "One of the things that often happens is that the incoming muddy water is warmer than the existing lake water, so initially it stays on the top. It shuts out light, which stops photosynthesis. This forces the baitfish up, so the bass follow.

"The key is timing. If lake conditions have been stable for several weeks and mud is suddenly washed in, the bass may actually stop biting for a day or so. That's when you look for clearer water.

"On the other hand, if the water has been muddy for a week or more and seems to be improving, you could be in for some surprising action. After they shut down for a day or so, bass usually start biting again with a vengeance.

"Initially, some bass may move ahead of incoming mud, again, I believe, because the bait is moving; but rarely have I ever seen a move of more than 50 or 75 yards. At some point the fish generally stop, usually in a little clearer water but often in a very small area like a tiny cove or mouth of a creek.

"The majority of bass don't really change locations, except to move up. They seem to adjust faster than fishermen do, and are often ready to bite again the next day."

Because muddy-water bass are usually very shallow, spinnerbaits have long been the favorite lure choice, especially those with large blades. But other lures work as well. Small, shallow-running crankbaits are excellent, especially if you can make them bounce and ricochet off limbs or rocks. A small lure like this won't dive under the bass, and the fish certainly don't seem to have any trouble finding it.

And don't overlook tiny hair jigs. A 1/8-ounce bucktail, marabou, or plastic jig on a spinning rod has often pulled bass out of shallow cover after I've worked the spots unsuccessfully with spinnerbaits and crankbaits.

TEMPERATURE CHANGE

RAPIDLY PLUNGING TEMPERATURES also can send bass quickly from the shallows to deeper water. We experience this every spring in the Deep South where bass are usually moving toward their spawning beds by mid-February.

"Normally, bass move out to the first breakline where the depth changes abruptly to deeper water," says Hawkes. "The fish suspend, and about all you can do is swim small worms, jigs, and grubs down through them.

"Remember, the baitfish are always more severely affected than the bass, and they move out first. You'll see them as solid masses on your depthfinder off the points or along the edges of the channel, and the bass will be underneath them."

On more shallow lakes, bass may move instead to heavy cover, especially if the front isn't quite as severe or if it's later in the year. In this case, what you need to change isn't *where* you're fishing, but *how* you're fishing. Start flipping small jigs and grubs in the brush and leave them down in the cover much longer than normal. You really have to work to make the fish bite. If you believe in scent attractors or noisy rattles for your lures, this is the time to use them.

Early autumn cold fronts, like rising water, bring fish up. The bass are preparing to move shallow anyway for their annual feeding binge, and a cold front that chills the water will hasten them. This is one reason fall fishing is some of the best of the year. A severe cold front at this time, however, acts like falling water, and will send the bass deep, sometimes for the entire winter.

Sometimes a midwinter warming trend, in which temperatures rise much higher than normal while the days remain sunny and bright, will warm water enough to bring deep bass more shallow. These fish will not come to the surface, but rather, suspend well above the bottom. On some lakes you'll find these fish hovering close to the sunny side of rock riprap, ridge abutments, or pier pilings.

The longer the weather remains warm, the more active these bass will become, so you can often fool them with a crankbait or a jig.

FLUCTUATING WATER LEVELS

CHANGING WATER LEVELS—rising or falling—generally pose a more serious problem, because these conditions nearly always make bass change locations. Basically, the rule of thumb to remember is that rising water pushes bass shallow, whereas falling water pulls them deeper.

"When I'm faced with rising water," says fellow tournament pro and guide Mike Hawkes, who often faces this condition on Texas' Lake Amistad and Lake Falcon where he guides, "I try to find the route they take to shallow water and simply follow them."

Hawkes simply picks an area he likes, such as a large bay or tributary river, and with his depthfinder, looks for a channel or ditch leading to shallow water. Often this channel will be intersected by other structure, such as a tree line or stump row, an old roadbed, or even a fence that will extend right to the shore. When Hawkes finds something like this, he simply fishes his way along it until he finds bass.

Lure choices for clear-rising water where bass may be skittish include small, lightly weighted plastic worms, quiet topwater plugs, small spinnerbaits, and one of the newer but smaller plastic jerkbaits. Slow retrieves are usually needed, too.

When the water is rising very rapidly, bass react a little differently. The rule here is to work the area between the old shoreline and the "new" one—the area of freshly flooded cover. Bass that were previously shallow usually come into the new cover almost immediately, but those in deeper water take their time about it; new bass are coming in continuously.

Just the opposite happens when water levels drop. As the shallow areas become more and more exposed, bass move into deeper water. Under these conditions, keep in mind the old saying, "Points point out fish."

"I look for those same migration routes bass might use when coming shallow, except this time I follow them in the opposite direction," says Hawkes.

"I really like little humps and saddles and other underwater features that are surrounded by deeper water. As with a slow rise of the water, you can also find bass really bunched in tight schools, and they're often really aggressive."

Many anglers get results by moving to the mouths of creeks when they encounter falling water conditions. They fish jigs, crankbaits, and plastic worms around the mouths of the tributaries.

Fishing changing water conditions can be a challenge, a valid reason for not catching fish. But with these tips, chances are you won't need any excuses, because no one has ever apologized for not getting skunked.

By Mark Hicks

Tactics for
STUBBORN BASS

WHEN THE FISH SEEM TO BE TAKING THE DAY OFF, THESE STRATEGIES WILL DELIVER A WAKE-UP CALL.

If they're convinced that a particular piece of cover or structure holds bass, they'll stay put and employ different strategies until the fish finally respond.

One effective stubborn-bass tactic is making repeated casts to the same spot, such as retrieving a buzzbait over a submerged treetop. Some experts believe this ploy aggravates the bass, while others feel it gradually arouses them from a neutral to an active state. The most difficult part of this ploy is maintaining concentration. Your mind will want to stray about the sixth time the lure sputters over the cover, and you may be looking elsewhere on cast number ten when an explosive strike serves as a rude wake-up call.

How many casts are sufficient? That depends on the bass and on how much confidence you have in the spot. Three casts would be a bare minimum, while a dozen casts or more would not be overdoing it in a prime location. Repetition also works well with spinnerbaits and rattling-type crankbaits.

When repeated casts with a noisy lure fail to initiate a strike, immediately follow up with a plastic worm. The commotion may have

THE HECTIC PACE OF the modern world has influenced bass fishing with high-performance boats, fast-retrieve reels, and lures that zip through the water. Supercharged anglers hit likely spots with one or two casts, then move on in search of other targets. This run-and-gun approach pays off when the fish are aggressive, but bass are more often reluctant biters that stubbornly refuse to be rushed.

A stubborn bass won't move far to intercept your offering, nor will it respond quickly—even when your presentation is right in its face. Many of the better bass anglers I have fished with, including noted tournament professionals, tend to be as muleheaded as the fish.

aroused the bass, but not enough to respond to a fast-paced presentation. A fake night crawler drifting slowly toward bottom, on the other hand, may serve as the final inducement that coaxes a bass into action. This scheme also works well over underwater structures, such as points, humps, and weedbeds.

Stubborn bass frequently show a preference for a specific retrieve angle, so it pays to cast from different positions. For example, if you've retrieved a spinnerbait past a stickup from right to left without results, position your boat on the other side of the stickup and try retrieving the spinnerbait from the opposite direction.

When fishing a dropoff with crankbaits, plastic worms, or some other lure, make sure you work it from positions that allow your lures to run downhill, uphill, and parallel to the dropoff. Don't be surprised if the bass find only one retrieve angle acceptable.

The trademark of a stubborn bass is its inflexibility regarding lure placement; either put your lures directly in front of the bass or go without strikes. Bass are especially bullheaded when holding tight in thick cover. This is when a long flippin' rod matched with a Texas-rigged worm or a hook-guard jig becomes invaluable. Heavy line should be used to extract bass from abrasive cover, preferably no less than 17-pound-test.

Methodically flip or pitch the lure into every opening, even though some may be no more than a foot apart. When fishing a windfall, treat each limb on both sides of the trunk as though it were an individual object. Fish tight to all sides of a stump, including the back, so as not to miss a single root. Probe every pothole and tiny opening in weedbeds, and every point and pocket along weed edges. The nook you miss may well be the one where a monster largemouth is lurking.

Bass in cover may engulf jigs or worms on the initial fall, but when they're in a finicky frame of mind, you'll need to drape and shake. To do this, drape the line over a twig, limb, root, or strand of vegetation—anything strong enough to hold the lure vertically in the cover. Let the lure sink a foot or more, depending on the depth of the water, and soak it for a few

seconds. Try to imagine that a bass is scrutinizing your lure and then twitch the rod tip once or twice to bring the lure to life. Immediately steady the rod and feel for the usually light tap that indicates a strike. On some days it may take several twitches to evoke a strike. Bass in cover typically hold the lure without swimming off, so don't wait for your line to move before setting the hook.

One of the most widely practiced stubborn bass maneuvers among skilled anglers is switching to smaller lures. One day the bass may be climbing over themselves to engulf a 7-inch plastic worm with a 1/4-ounce slip sinker. Overnight, the bass change their mood from tenacious to tentative, due to the passage of a cold front, increased fishing pressure, heavy boat traffic, or some other mysterious malady. The next day you get fewer bites on the same lure in the same places, and you can't hook those that do grab the worm.

You'll get more strikes by replacing the larger worm with a 4-inch model and dropping from a 1/4-ounce sinker to an 1/8- or 1/16-ounce weight. The same strategy applies to jigs, such as dropping from a 3/8-ounce jig tipped with a large pork frog to a 3/16-ounce jig tipped with a smaller, spinning-size pork frog. Stubborn bass respond better to smaller lures and, while they still expend less energy during the strike, they are more likely to completely inhale lighter worms and jigs, improving your odds for solid hookups.

Most anglers avoid tiny worms and jigs because lighter lures are more difficult to work with, especially when you must place them precisely into small openings in dense cover. With practice, however, you can master the techniques for tossing diminutive offerings, and you'll often find yourself catching bass when anglers fishing nearby with larger lures are having little success.

Another tactic for coaxing reluctant bass is the bump and run, which involves bumping crankbaits into submerged stumps, logs, rocks, and other cover to trigger bass into striking. It also pays to bump spinnerbaits into stumps and logs, as well as into emergent vegetation, such as reeds, lily pads, and bulrushes. The bump and run is nothing new, but many anglers forget to try it when bass grow stubborn.

An offshoot of the bump and run could be called the dip and rip, because it is used over submerged vegetation such as hydrilla and milfoil. The top of the weeds may be anywhere from a foot to several feet deep, and when bass are aggressive you can easily induce strikes by retrieving lures in the open water above the vegetation. Uncooperative bass, however, settle down into the greenery and require prodding.

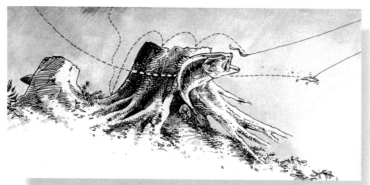

Sometimes a noise-making lure, such as a rattling crankbait, will arouse bass, but not enough to make them strike. Immediately following a noisy lure with a slow, silent plastic worm can serve as the clincher.

Uncooperative largemouths that settle into vegetation require extra prodding. This dip-and-rip tactic will do the job. Simply allow your lure to dip down and touch the weed tops, then rip it sharply through the greenery.

Lipless rattling crankbaits, heavy big-bladed spinnerbaits, and hook-guard jigs with large pork or plastic trailers work well here. Allow these lures to dip down and make contact with the weed tops and then pop them through the vegetation with a sharp upward snap of the rod tip. This is when bass fishing becomes a contact sport. A stiff, graphite rod will help the lures break cleanly through the weeds. The sudden burst when the lure breaks free is just what it takes to spark a reflex strike from a bass.

When fishing submerged weeds, and virtually any type of bass cover and structure, the bow-mounted electric motor has proven to be the optimum tool for boat positioning. As a result, few bass anglers these days consider fishing from an anchored boat, though anchoring is sometimes the best technique for stubborn bass. Fighting wind, waves, or strong currents with an electric motor is difficult, tiring, and often ineffective when working around cover and structure.

Anchoring maintains the boat in proper position and lets you fish silently and effortlessly. A key place to anchor is on the inside turn of a weed line, since this is where stubborn bass tend to congregate. Idle the boat well upwind of the area you would like to fish before dropping anchor. When the anchor takes hold, feed rope until the boat is positioned correctly. Tie the anchor rope to the bow, preferably to the bow eye, for the least resistance and to prevent waves from washing in. A second anchor dropped off the stern will prevent the boat from drifting back and forth.

Staying put in an anchored boat allows you to keep your lures in front of the bass. You may have to wait an hour between strikes when bass are stubborn, but you'll fare better than anglers who are being pushed about by the wind and who eventually end up with dead electric motor batteries at midday.

Whether fishing submerged weeds, structures, or visible objects, you'll have to rely on intuition concerning how long to stay with a particular location. Active bass quickly reveal their presence, while laid-back, finicky fish require patience. In most situations the bass aren't going anywhere, and neither should you. The key to success lies in being more stubborn than the fish.

By Ken Schultz

The DAWN PATROL

THE BEST WARM-WEATHER BASS FISHING IS LIKELY TO HAPPEN IN THE MAGIC HOURS BETWEEN THE COMING OF THE FIRST FAINT LIGHT AND THE MOMENT THE SUN RISES ABOVE THE TREES.

FOR BASS ANGLERS there is no finer time to fish than a spring or summer dawn when the day is windless, the sky cloudless, and mist rests on the still water. In the cool freshness of early morning, anything seems possible—and as far as bass fishing goes, it probably is, for the best action of the day often occurs before the sun rises 45 degrees above the horizon.

I first started bass fishing years ago on a municipal water supply reservoir that did not allow motors. I kept a leaky wooden rowboat along one shore, and I would usually arrive as the blackness of night was fading to an only slightly lighter gray. There was a rich pine smell where I kept the boat, and it seemed that a crow or two always called loudly as I made my way to the edge of the water.

The surface of the reservoir was usually calm on those summer mornings, and there was a nearby weedbed dropoff that I would row to. I frequently caught smallmouth bass of about 3 pounds at that spot, using an old

lure called a Gudebrod Sinner Spinner, a surface plug shaped like a small cigar with fore-and-aft propellers. For a long while, every good catch was made between 6 and 6:15 in the morning, and if I overslept and got to the water later than that, I felt that I had wasted my time.

There are a number of reasons why it's smart to fish for bass at first light. The fish are more likely to be shallow; to be active; and to be caught on surface lures. Moreover, the fish have not been disturbed by boaters, skiers, or other anglers; and many fishermen are sharper and more attuned to their surroundings, able to integrate with them and take advantage of this heightened opportunity.

To best capitalize on these positive points, you have to be on the water just as it is getting light. In my experience, the dark hours of early morning do not usually bring good fishing. Perhaps I'm missing something, but for me, the magic time has arrived when I can make out objects along shore or in the water well enough to cast to them.

This is especially true in late spring and summer. In the early spring, especially in northern waters, when the water is still cold at first light, you're better off waiting till the end of the day when the water has been warmed several degrees by the sun. But in the warm months, when the surface and shallows are cooled by darkness, the best time for bass is the first hour of daylight. As soon as the sun peeks over the trees and starts the warming process, the opportunities start to fade.

For anyone who likes fishing with surface lures, first light is prime time. During the bright light and heat of midday, surface lures are usually not as productive as other types. When skies are overcast or the light is dim, bass respond better to surface lures. The possibility of catching big bass also increases at this time, in part because surface lures are usually large and appear to be a formidable meal.

Walking plugs such as a Zara Spook or Rogers Jim Dandy are my favorite choice for big bass and low-light angling. When retrieved properly they have a subtle but naturally attractive action and sound. They can be cast a long way for working open areas (such as over the tops of submerged grass), and they are especially effective on sharply sloping points and around logs, docks, standing timber, and bushes, all of which are typical ambush cover for largemouth bass. They are also good around vegetation, but in heavy cover you might find it better to use a weedless surface lure.

My second choice, but often a more productive surface lure than others, is a stick or minnow-style bait with a propeller on the rear. Bagley's Bang-O-Lure with spinner was the only lure of this kind for years, but Rebel now has one, although I have not fished it.

There are a lot of multiple propeller plugs around, and many of these are also effective, but the Bang-O-Lure is different because it has a small diving lip as well as a single rear propeller, and the lure swims as well as rips when it is jerked. It is not a profound noisemaker, but has a more subtle sound. It is effective on calm and rippling water, in all of the normal bass haunts, and it has two other characteristics of note.

One is that it often works when other surface lures don't, and in places that are fished hard or where there is a lot of daytime activity. Bass, especially largemouths, are thought of as a fairly aggressive freshwater fish, but they aren't always that way. Bass that are spooky—for whatever reason—are not very aggressive. These fish need subtle, slow presentations. A really noisy lure, or one that is worked quickly, like a spinnerbait or buzzbait, may be spurned.

The other notable characteristic about this type of lure is that it catches smallmouth bass just as well as largemouths. Smallmouths have to be really charged up to take a large surface lure, and though they will do this in the spring when they are shallow and in a spawning stage, they are not always this aggressive. But they will respond at other times to a minnow plug (with or without a propeller) worked slowly in early morning, even one that is 5 inches long, which is substantial for a smallmouth.

There are other lures, of course, that will catch first-light fish. When bass are aggressive and taking well, almost any type of lure will produce. Generally, however, spinnerbaits are extremely effective, especially in spring (and early summer in the North), and shallow or medium-running crankbaits work well, too. When you are fishing the shallows, you don't need deep divers, but being versatile may pay off.

Bass are more active in early morning, but they aren't pushovers.

A few years ago, on Lake Eufaula in Alabama, a friend and I visited a spot where he thought we might catch early morning largemouths. It was perhaps 10 feet deep and over an old roadbed where there had been a culvert. He suggested using a lipless shallow-swimming plug, which we did for a while, catching one or two small bass. After a time, just to see what would happen, I changed to a deep-diving plug and caught a 5-pound largemouth. My friend remembered that incident in later weeks and returned to the spot with the same deep-running lure. He caught enough bass to win or place highly in several tournaments.

Crankbaits may be effective in the dawn hours on a steady retrieve, but stop-and-go retrieval is often more productive early in the spring when the water is cool and fish swipe at lures to stun them. This characteristic behavior of bass in cool water, incidentally, results in a lot of "taps," which are near misses or feint strikes. Using a trailer hook on a spinnerbait helps catch short-strikers, but you should generally watch your lures carefully when they are retrieved. If you see or feel strikes that do not result in hookups, change the cadence of your retrieve. Slow it down, and use a stop-and-go movement. Sharpen your hooks, too, because many such fish are barely hooked, and a dull or round point will not hold them.

It also pays to be quiet when fishing at first light. Usually, there is little or no wind at dawn to create a ripple on the surface and muffle sounds, so it pays to use stealth and stalk bass rather than bluster into them.

Some anglers underestimate the sensitivity of a bass, perhaps because of the cover or the murkiness of the water the fish often inhabit. Being quiet is important in a lot of areas that are heavily fished and where many bass have been caught and released. These are not stupid creatures, and they can make associations. Don't knock around in the boat, shuffle a tackle box across a bare aluminum floor, bang objects on the gunwales, and so forth. It may also be beneficial to use the electric motor on low power and sparingly, and to cut your out-board a reasonable distance from the place you want to fish. The main point is not to be unnecessarily alarming.

What are the places to focus on in the early hours? There's no end to the possibilities. But to narrow the field a bit, here are a few things to key on.

If you have been fishing the previous day or in recent days and caught bass in a given area, that place would be a good starting spot for the morning, as would all places where you caught bass recently. Remember that at first light bass may be more active and accessible than at other times, so it may be a good idea to check out a few places quickly rather than spend a long time at one. If you have seen or lost a big bass in a particular spot, that would obviously be worth visiting at first light.

Being observant will pay off, too. Look for disturbances in the water where bait is riled or where a bass has swirled after striking prey. Such things are more likely to be observed early in the day than later.

Where there is a lot of cover, try working the edges and the places that are different from the rest of the cover, perhaps a pocket or point in vegetation, or the tip or edge of a cluster of timber. Lone objects like a large stump or fallen log are very worthwhile, and may be the most likely spots of all to harbor bigger fish.

On a small lake that I used to fish often, starting at first light, there was a small bay where the boats were put in and which lead to the wider part of the lake. It was a heavily weeded lake, and in the middle of that bay in about 9 feet of water was a big old log with moss on it, at a 30-degree angle out of the water. Almost everyone would pass by that log to work the thickly covered shoreline, which often produced quite a few bass. I usually fished the shoreline, too, but I never passed up that log, even though forty-nine times out of fifty I caught nothing there. But when it did pay off, it paid off big: on one early morning it produced a 7-pound largemouth and on another a 6-pounder—an excellent reward for working the dawn patrol.

By Mark Hicks

The EDGE of NIGHT

WHEN LOW LIGHT
PREVAILS, BASS PROWL
WITH ABANDON, AND
THEIR HEARTY
APPETITES GUARANTEE
HEART-STOPPING
STRIKES.

YOU MAY NOT BE BIG
on soap operas, but every
bass fisherman should tune into "the
edge of night." When dim light prevails, bass
prowl and are more susceptible to an angler's
offerings. If your senses don't awaken during
those magical hours of dawn and dusk, you've
been away from the water too long.

While the edge of night may come
through in any season, it is especially produc-

Preparing for the Night Shift

silently through the darkness and make long casts catch more bass. Have two or three rods rigged with different lures, so you don't waste time and create a disturbance bumbling through a tackle box. Boating fishermen should use their electric motors or paddles sparingly, and those casting from shore should take pains to step lightly.

Preparations for fishing the edge of night should be the same as for night fishing, since you'll be traveling to and from fishing locations in the dark. A penlight serves well for locating lures and tying knots, and consider painting the lens red, since this color least affects night vision. A flashlight or spotlight will help you get where you're going. Remember to bring insect repellent and carry a net even if you don't use one during the day. Trying to hand-land bass in faint light invites lacerations.

Boating anglers should check running lights before leaving the ramp. If you don't already have a compass for navigation, install one. It will more than pay for itself the first time you become disoriented or engulfed in fog. Familiarize yourself with strange lakes during the day and slow down when darkness envelops you.

Even though bass don't see as well in the twilight, their ability to detect sounds and vibrations is unhampered. These senses may be even more acute, because the bass are relying on them more to find and capture forage. Noisy, overzealous anglers alarm fish and drive them away. Fishermen who skulk

tive when spring gives way to summer, and feeding, rather than spawning, becomes the primary focus for bass. The fish begin frequenting their favorite eateries on daily schedules, and the table is usually set for hearty appetites when the light is low.

In the evening, baitfish come up near the surface to feed on microorganisms and newly hatched insects. Crayfish, which are nocturnal, begin creeping out from protective niches on the bottom. Bass, keenly aware of these movements, venture into the gloom, which veils their presence and helps them take advantage of their prey. The initial assault is worth waiting for. The feeding goes on sporadically throughout the night and usually intensifies as dawn approaches, because bass know this is their last opportunity to fill their bellies under the protective cover of night.

Stable weather favorably influences twi-

light binges, and unforgettable action may be in store when a major lunar feeding period coincides with the half light. Even when cold fronts undermine feeding activity, you may enjoy brief periods of fast fishing early and late that provide most or all of the action for an entire day on the water.

Faint-light fishing is productive on all but the dingiest bass waters, but it pays off best on clear lakes, ponds, and reservoirs. Clear-water bass become more reclusive when the sun shines, burrowing in weeds or dense wood cover, or swimming off into deeper, open water and suspending above the bottom. Inactive, suspended bass are the most difficult to catch, and those hiding in the thick stuff are no picnic, either. Their bad attitude gets even worse when pleasant weather brings forth throngs of fishermen and water worshipers who froth the surface. On lakes with heavy traffic, the fishing may be at its worst just prior to sunset. When the sky darkens, the throngs retreat, the water calms, and the bass become aggressive.

Bass in clear, heavily fished environments spurn many lures that look obviously fraudulent under the hard light of day, particularly large spinnerbaits, crankbaits, and topwater plugs. When obscured by the gloom, however, these same lures tempt bass with subdued flashes and subtle silhouettes. You also may use heavier lines, say 12- to 17-pound-test.

Lures that cover a lot of water improve your odds for finding active fish. Big-bladed spinnerbaits in the 1/2-ounce class serve well. A single, large Colorado blade churns with a distinctive throb that helps you keep track of the lure and detect strikes. A silver blade with a black head and skirt is a proven combination. The entire gamut of topwater lures is deadly in dim light, including buzzbaits, poppers, propeller baits, dog-walkers, wobblers, and floating minnows (including jointed models). Retrieve these lures with a consistent cadence to help the bass zero in on them.

Fat crankbaits with wide wobbles also tempt strikes in the twilight. Shallow, medium, and deep divers will earn their keep, since not all bass move shallow in pale light. Slow, steady bottom-ticking retrieves work well, especially if you pause after making solid bottom contact. Sometimes burning the lures down and stopping them abruptly also triggers strikes. As with all bass fishing, you must match the lure to the location.

Twilight bass relate to many typical covers and structures that you normally would fish under sunlight. A spot that fails to produce a single strike at midday may yield several bites when the light wanes. At these times bass usually move shallower, relate loosely to cover, and often linger over barren structures that wouldn't hold them long during daylight hours.

Bass in submerged weeds, for example, move out from the thickest portions and deep edges at twilight and cruise freely over the vegetation. Points, ridges, and edges of weeds are the most likely producers, especially points that often attract schools of bass. Retrieving a spinnerbait steadily over the weeds or working your favorite topwater lure should find ready takers. The same lures are effective when fished along the edges of lily pads and matted or emergent weeds at these times.

A bass relating to wood cover, such as a bushy fallen tree, may be in solitary confinement under a maze of limbs when the sun is bright. Fading light sets the bass free, allowing it to move up and roam about over the branches. Cast a spinnerbait or topwater lure beyond the fish and retrieve it over the cover. Don't be concerned with penetrating the cover, because the bass will be drawn up to your lure. Also fish the banks nearby, since the bass may be cruising in search of food.

Suspended bass in open water move up on points and humps during low light and, here again, spinnerbaits and topwater lures are effective, provided the bass are in the shallows or feeding near the surface. If the bass are bottom feeding in deeper water, get down to them with a diving crankbait or by fishing a spinnerbait with a lift-drop retrieve. After the spinnerbait sinks to the bottom, sweep it up by lifting the rod tip from about 9 o'clock to 11 o'clock and letting the lure flutter back to the bottom on a tight line. Most strikes occur as the spinnerbait falls.

Because the edge of night passes quickly, it is imperative that you spend this time fishing key locations rather than randomly casting down a bank. Hit the spot you feel has the greatest potential first—go for the throat. If the fish are present, they'll probably keep you busy throughout the twilight. If bites are not soon in coming, jump to another nearby primary area. Sometimes the evening feed will continue for two or three hours into the night. This is when it pays to fish secondary areas and have an understanding spouse.

As good as twilight fishing can be, it remains relatively unpressured. Most anglers fail to rise early enough or are unwilling to stay out late enough to take advantage of the edge of night. You'd be wise to tune in regularly, however, because it's worth not missing a single episode.

By Joe Doggett

UNLIKELY ALLIES

IF BASS FISHING CONDITIONS LIKE HIGH WIND, MUDDY RUNOFFS, AND THICK WEEDS AREN'T YOUR IDEA OF A GOOD TIME, THEN MAYBE YOUR IDEA OF A GOOD TIME DOESN'T INVOLVE CATCHING FISH.

THE LAUNCH RAMP AT Fayette County Lake was empty. I wasn't surprised. Scudding clouds and pummeling gusts had made a shambles of the February forecast, and the gray water of the open lake was torn by chops. Even the small cove facing the ramp was tattered.

Not the kind of day when you'd just drop everything and grab a bass rod. Or would you?

Guide Gene Ballard was waiting in his vehicle—a big Suburban, a no-nonsense rig typical of those used by touring bass pros in Texas. The empty boat trailer dripped impatiently. The driver's window hummed down, trailing a two-step twang and a curl of coffee steam. "You're late," he said.

"Sorry, I got tangled up getting out of Houston."

"At least you're here; my first party canceled." The pro snorted. "They said the weather was looking too rough. I tried to tell 'em but—oh, never mind. Let's hit it; I've got the boat tied off below."

Five hours later we returned, spray-lashed but beaming over a slam-bam session that yielded twenty-five or thirty bass, all solid fish between 2 and 5 pounds. Most were taken on spinnerbaits and soft jerkbaits worked amid the choppy shallows of an exposed shoreline. Keeping the boat in position with the troll motor was the biggest problem the guide faced—other than losing those balky clients.

What Ballard had tried to "tell 'em" was that the early-season south wind was not a problem but an asset. It was one of several apparent setbacks that actually can improve fishing. Here are three of the bass angler's unlikely allies:

HIGH WIND

NOT JUST ANY wind will work; during early season look for a mild and balmy influence from the southerly quadrant rather than the withering blast of a cold front. A muggy south wind may create gloomy, rough conditions, but the sustained warmth will jack both air and water temperatures and supercharge the shallows.

A rise of only a few degrees can make a big difference in the aggressiveness of fish getting ready to spawn; for this reason, the exposed shorelines that catch the warming influence can be most productive.

Temperatures aside, a wind-blown bank can be an advantage at any time of the year. The sustained movement of chops and currents piling into an exposed shoreline stirs and oxygenates that belt of shallow water. The same influence can push random forage and stack the bounty along the windward banks. This combination of agitated water and available forage is an attractive draw in any season for aggressive bass in a healthy lake.

Also, wind provides a reassuring measure of "cover." Bass in shallow water might be predatory, prowling the edges or lurking in ambush, but high-visibility conditions make them skittish. A calm, slick surface might appear promising to a fisherman, but to a bass it magnifies the vulnerability of the shallows. Conversely, rolling chops and riffles break images and create reassuring confusion. The garbled shadows encourage fish to move with abandon.

At the same time, the ally of a wind-whipped surface helps mask the angler's approach and presentation. Casting performance is improved with a tail wind, and imitation bait trailing gleaming hooks and twirling blades becomes more believable.

MUDDY RUNOFFS

DIRTY WATER IS depressing. No question, a sudden flush of reddish brown or chalky gray water can dampen enthusiasm for fishing in even the most celebrated lake. Resident bass, however, are stuck with the turbid water. They make the best of the situation. So can you.

Timing is important. During the onset of a runoff, the worst of conditions usually start in the upper reaches of a watershed. Despite "bad press," the lower portions of a big lake can stay wide open, untouched by the mud for maybe hours, days, or weeks. . . it's hard to say. But, depending on the conditions, the fisherman who stays on top of the situation can take advantage of the good water while the boo-birds sulk at home.

Of course, a major runoff eventually will impact an entire lake. During a heavy influx, the main arteries—the primary rivers and creeks that feed the lake—will be carrying most of the off-color flow. At a glance, as you cross a bridge, the lake looks terrible. However, the savvy angler can dodge the worst of the dirty water by fishing coves and sloughs buffered from the main flow. Many such possibilities exist on the typical bass reservoir.

The water in these select areas still may be murky, but the clarity almost certainly will be noticeably superior to that of the main-stream runoffs. A measure of off-color water is not all bad; indeed, a murky rise can solidly improve bass fishing. Shallow bass gain confidence in off-color water. As with a wind-whipped surface, the reduced visibility of murky water provides cover and the rising level associated with the runoffs encourages bass to move to the shallows. As long as the water maintains a foot or so of subsurface visibility, conditions are excellent for banging the brush.

Shallow bass holding amid thick cover in murky water are ambush feeders. They react to sound as well as sight, and the strikes on close-passing chances are reflexive and vicious. Further-more, the fish are slow to spook. This arrogance favors an aggressive approach. You can press fish by using the reduced visibility as a cushion. Even sloppy casting can be forgiven; indeed, the nearby smack of a careless lure might actually summon a fish lurking in the gloom.

THICK WEEDS

BASS AND BRUSH go together like cigars and poker chips, but some anglers are discouraged by overwhelming weed growth. Mats of surface vegetation can choke access to many coves and banks, restricting the fishable water and creating ongoing hassles when maneuvering and casting. Despite these problems, aquatic vegetation provides several advantages for bass fishermen. The canopies of shade maintain cooler temperatures during hot weather, and the photosynthesis can reoxygenate stale water. A dense top-to-bottom weed mat rimming a cove or ridge can serve as a blocking and filtering system to maintain clear water against passing sediments (a key to remember during runoffs). Also, thick surface mats and stalks increase the forage base by attracting ter-restrial prey such as frogs and dragonflies, or even small turtles and snakes. Bass are oppor-tunistic feeders, and rich weed growth can offer a smorgasbord lacking in open water.

Finally, to an old plugger, weeds just look good. The dropoff edge of a lily field or a pocket in the coontail whispers "big bass" and begs for a cast. So does that stand of cattails in the back of the cove. There's nothing like chunking at a bunch of fresh "green stuff" to raise the optimism in a sagging bass boat. Open water gets boring fast.

Most veteran bass busters would agree that too many weeds are better than too few. No lure is truly weedless and tossing a green salad can be frustrating and annoying, but aquatic vege-tation reaches to the core of bass fishing. No matter how clogged the lake may appear, edges of opportunity are there for the determined angler to check out. If nothing else, weeds teach the traditional values of accurate casting.

Wind, mud, and weeds are all apparent setbacks that can be made to benefit the tuned-in bass angler. The ability to turn a negative into a positive is a trump on any hard-fished bass lake. The angler who utilizes these unlike-ly allies can increase his success as well as get a jump on the competition—the "other guy," who, more often than the weather, can be the major obstacle on public water.

Author Biographies

Philip Bourjaily caught his first farm pond fish at the age of 6. Today, he is a Contributing Editor for FIELD & STREAM. Co-author (with his father, novelist Vance Bourjaily) of the book, *Fishing by Mail*, he is also Ducks Unlimited's 1997 Wetlands Conservation Achievement Award Winner.

Wade L. Bourne is a writer/broadcaster who has covered bass fishing in North America for more than 20 years. He hosts *Advantage Outdoors TV* on The Nashville Network, produces the nationally syndicated *In-Fisherman Radio* show, and writes for numerous outdoor magazines.

Bob Brister may be best known as a leading authority on shotguns; he is also an accomplished bass fisherman. During his 40 years as Outdoors Editor for the *Houston Chronicle*, Brister (who has also served as FIELD & STREAM's Shooting Editor) often wrote about the sporting qualities of the largemouth bass.

Bryon W. Dalrymple's articles appeared in FIELD & STREAM from 1945 through 1994. He always retained his enthusiasm for fishing, hunting and travel, as well as for writing about them, until his death in 1994.

Jim Dean has been writing articles for FIELD & STREAM and other major outdoor magazines for 35 years. He recently retired from his position as Editor of *Wildlife in North Carolina* to write full-time.

Joe Doggett has been an outdoor writer for the *Houston Chronicle* for the last 25 years. He is also a Contributing Editor for FIELD & STREAM. Joe is recognized as a world-class multi-species angler in both fresh and salt water.

Cliff Hauptman has had hundreds of fishing articles published in most of the major outdoor magazines. He is the author of several books on fishing, including *The Flyfisher's Guide to Warmwater Lakes* and a novel, *The Dog-Nose Chronicles*. Cliff is Director of Publications at Brandeis University.

Mark Hicks, an award-winning writer, photographer and book author, has been a regular contributor to FIELD & STREAM for nearly 20 years. He has qualified three times for the prestigious B.A.S.S. Top 100 tournament circuit and once for the Red Man All-American. He also writes under the pen name Glenn Edwards.

Nick Lyons is the author of 18 books and hundreds of articles, most of them on fishing. He is the founder and publisher of The Lyons Press.

Keith McCafferty is a Contributing Editor for FIELD & STREAM. His articles have been published in many literary and outdoor magazines. Keith is the author of *The L.L. Bean Guide to Family Camping* and *The L.L. Bean Guide to Hiking, Backpacking and Camping*.

W. Hardbark McLoughlin is a well-known humor writer and illustrator. He is a Contributing Editor for FIELD & STREAM and has written humor pieces for *Sports Afield*, *Playboy* and *Esquire*. His illustrated children's books include *Voices of the Wild* and *Master Elk & the Mountain Lion*.

John Merwin, a Contributing Editor for FIELD & STREAM, is the author and/or editor of more than 15 books on sportfishing.

Doug Pike has been an outdoor columnist at the *Houston Chronicle* for 15 years. In addition, he is Editor of the Coastal Conservation Association's TIDE magazine and Regional Editor for FIELD & STREAM.

Steve Price has been an outdoor writer for more than 25 years, during which time his articles and photographs have appeared in more than 2,000 magazine articles and numerous books. He served as the South Regional Editor for FIELD & STREAM from 1985 to 1992.

Ken Schultz, a Contributing Editor and staff fishing writer for FIELD & STREAM for over 25 years, occasionally writes for the Sunday Sports section of *The New York Times*. He's the author of a dozen books on sportfishing techniques and travel.

Bill Volkart is an avid angler and freelance writer based in southern Ohio. He has fished the waters of the Midwest and Canada for over 40 years. Bill's work has appeared regularly in national and regional outdoor publications since 1987.

Slaton L. White joined FIELD & STREAM in 1981 as an Associate Editor. He became Managing Editor in 1995. He has fished for largemouth bass throughout their range for more than 20 years.

Photo Credits

Photographers

Joe Albea
Greenville, NC
© Joe Albea: p. 50

Grady Allen
El Campo, TX
© Grady Allen: p. 157

Bob Brister
Houston, TX
© Bob Brister: pp. 17, 18

Jim Dean
Raleigh, NC
© Jim Dean: p. 60

Joe Doggett
Houston, TX
© Joe Doggett: p. 38

Mark Hicks
Millfield, OH
© Mark Hicks: pp. 88 both, 153

Bill Lindner
Minneapolis, MN
© Bill Lindner: cover

David J. Sams/Texas Inprint
Dallas, TX
© David J. Sams/Texas Inprint: pp. 23, 24, 25 both, 26, 55

Ken Schultz
Forestburgh, NY
© Ken Schultz: pp. 33, 150

Dave Whitlock
Midway, AR
© Dave Whitlock: p. 84 all

Illustrators

John F. Eggert
Marstons Mills, MA
© John F. Eggert: pp. 58, 59 all, 89, 107, 114, 118, 143, 144, 145

Dale Glasgow & Associates
Fredricksburg, VA
© Dale Glasgow & Associates: back cover, p. 49

W. Hardbark McLoughlin
Bellows Falls, VT
© Wayne McLoughlin: pp. 8-9, 14, 31

Doug Schermer
Peoria, IL
© Doug Schermer: p. 148 both

Slim Films
New York, NY
© Slim Films: p. 45 both